SPIRITUAL

ZEST

FINDING IT
&
KEEPING IT

SPIRITUAL ZEST

FINDING IT

&

KEEPING IT

Though this book is designed for group study, it is also intended for your personal enjoyment and spiritual growth. A leader's guide is available from your local bookstore or from your publisher.

Beacon Hill Press of Kansas City
Kansas City, Missouri

Editor
Stephen M. Miller

Editorial Assistant
Rebecca Privett

Editorial Committee
Randy Cloud
Thomas Mayse
Stephen M. Miller
Carl Pierce
Rebecca Privett
Gene Van Note

Copyright 1993
Beacon Hill Press of Kansas City
Kansas City, Mo.
Printed in the United States of America
ISBN 083-411-4488

Cover design by Paul Franitza

Back cover cartoon by Doug Hall

10   9   8   7   6   5   4

Contents

1

Ten Questions to Ask
When Your Spiritual Life Is Dull and Dry

by Jean Fleming

NEARLY ALL OF US experience times when our spiritual appetites diminish or when God seems distant. These "seasons" can be discouraging, distressing, or even downright frightening.

How do we get through them?

The following 10 questions provide some basic ideas to help us understand, interpret, and grow—even in a spiritual desert.

1. Are my expectations unrealistic?

A man deeply committed to Christ wept as he told my husband about his concern for the condition of his own spiritual life. As my husband probed further, he began to wonder if our friend had an unrealistic picture of what our life in Christ should look like.

It's easy to do. Biographies often depict the most dramatic and glowing incidents from the subject's life. We read that David Brainerd, a pioneer missionary to the American Indians in the 1700s, knelt in the snow for hours to pray for the Native Americans he was trying to reach for

Christ. But we gloss over the sections that tell of his bouts with melancholia.

Even in the life of King David, as recorded in the Old Testament, we tend to overlook the times that he didn't sense the presence of God. Yet the historical accounts of his life, as well as his songs, show David experienced times of doubt and spiritual coldness (Psalm 13). However, the touchstone of David's life is not primarily that he always walked in the full enjoyment of God's presence, but that even in dry times he trusted in God.

2. Is there any sin I need to confess to God and turn from?

Half-buried sin does great harm. It stamps down the soil of our lives, making it as hard and impenetrable as an ancient path, so that God's words to us, His advances, and the prompting of His Spirit cannot pierce its surface. David knew this, and his words are recorded in Psalm 139:23-24: "Search me, O God, and know my heart; test me and know my anxious thoughts. See if there is any offensive way in me, and lead me in the way everlasting."

The desire to turn from our sin is the heart of repentance. This desire was the difference between Saul and David. Both sinned. Both confessed. But the similarity ends there. Saul confessed his sin, hoping to retain a position of prominence. David lamented his sin because it was an offense to God.

Hypocrisy devastates our spiritual lives, so periodically we need to examine our lives to see if they match our spiritual talk.

3. Am I engaged in practices that dull my spiritual sensitivity?

Susanna Wesley, mother of Methodist founders John and Charles Wesley, told her children that anything that dulled their desire for God was sin for them. Hebrews 12:1

says it this way: "Let us throw off everything that hinders . . . and let us run with perseverance the race marked out for us."

This is largely an individual matter linked to our consciences. Each of us must develop discernment and sensitivity to the areas that may hinder our walk with Christ, whether it is movies, books, television, music, or unhealthy relationships.

Luke 8:14 warns us that "life's worries, riches and pleasures" choke God's Word in our lives. Stress, anxiety, preoccupation, time pressures, distorted values, and poor choices can strangle our life in Christ.

4. Am I consistent in spiritual disciplines?

I meet people who recoil at the mention of spiritual disciplines because they fear legalism. Faithfulness in spiritual disciplines should not be confused with legalism.

Spiritual discipline does not gain Christ's love or favor. Rather, the benefit lies in helping us focus on the grace and nearness of God and on His love and commitment to us. This means making a deliberate choice to spend time with Him, because what is real, true, and supremely important is invisible and never pressing.

5. What conditions surrounded my best times with the Lord?

Revelation 2:5a gives the prescription for regaining first love: "Remember the height from which you have fallen! Repent and do the things you did at first."

Jesus calls us to remember the high points, the times of greatest reality and joy in our relationship with Him. We refresh ourselves with the memory of the attitudes, actions, and thoughts that predominated during that period.

For example, in my best times with the Lord I was very aware of my need and His sufficiency. So when I find myself in a dry time, I sometimes use this helpful exercise:

I list my needs and His ability to provide what is needed. As I list my need for wisdom, humility, or courage and consider His rich promises, my heart is warmed.

After I ponder the memory of my high points with Christ, He tells me to contemplate the height from which I have fallen. Where am I now compared to then? I consider the past heights that I might repent. Perhaps I need to ask forgiveness for living as if I were self-sufficient or for not taking the time to consider what my current needs are and how God can meet them. Or perhaps my need is to cultivate those courting rituals that sweethearts know so well.

After I remember the height from which I have fallen and I repent, then God tells me to recover past practices. He says, "Do the things you did at first." First love—the fervent love of a bride and bridegroom for each other—is expressed in "first things." If you sang spontaneously to the Lord, then sing again.

Bride love is a love of abandonment. In Jeremiah 2:2 the Lord says, "I remember . . . how as a bride you loved me and followed me through the desert." The purest expression of first love is unmitigated joy in being near Him, regardless of the conditions.

6. Have I fallen into a spiritual rut?

Writer George MacDonald said, "Nothing is so deadening to the divine as a habitual dealing with the outsides of holy things." Do you attend church? You should. But perhaps you need to rethink why you do. Do you read the Bible and pray? Maybe you need to examine your motivations to see if you've lost sight of the true goal of these activities.

Disciplines that should breathe the very life of God into our lives can stiffen in rigor mortis if we lose sight of Christ himself. We must meet with a Person, not a habit.

We all know married couples whose conversation

with each other seldom reaches beyond the exchange of functional information or the rehashing of the same events or thoughts. In our relationship with God, we can fall into similar patterns.

It has helped me to expand the dimensions of my time with God by meeting with Him around different issues. Often He chooses the issues as He speaks through the Bible or to my mind by His Holy Spirit. In these times, He may convict me of lying, or He may instruct me about love.

Sometimes *I* raise the topic of conversation. For example, I may read John 3:16 to consider His grace or His mercy, the cost to God as Father, the cost to God as Son, or what is the essence of this giving. This kind of interaction with God could go on and on as we contemplate a well-known verse from different angles.

Another approach is to sing psalms to the Lord or come into His presence as you might come into your boss's office for the day's instructions.

7. Is poor health or fatigue a factor?

Elijah was depressed, ready to give up, to lie down and die (1 Kings 19:4). What he did, however, was to lie down and sleep. One has only to read 1 Kings 18:16-46 to understand the tremendous spiritual, mental, physical, and emotional exertion Elijah had expended.

God didn't chide Elijah for his despondency. He sent an angel to fix Elijah breakfast twice and to tuck him in.

Don't assume that spiritual dryness is a spiritual problem. Fatigue, chemical imbalance, or illness can impair your judgment. A friend or doctor may more objectively discern your need.

8. Am I praying for God's blessing on my life and enlisting the prayers of others?

Wouldn't you think a guy whose mother named him

"pain" would be at a disadvantage in life? Yet God said that Jabez (which sounds like the Hebrew word for pain) was more honorable than his brothers because he begged God to bless him, to enlarge his territory, and to keep him free from pain (1 Chronicles 4:9-10).

What are you praying for yourself? Ask God to make His presence real to you, His Word rich and alive, and His ways clear. Ask God to give you a responsive heart.

Sometimes during dry times I depend on the prayers of others. Like the paralyzed man who allowed others to present his need to Jesus (Matthew 9:2), I ask others to pray that God would sustain me and draw me into the warmth of His presence again.

9. What person or group might stimulate my life in Christ?

Ecclesiastes 4:9-12 says, "Two are better than one, because they have a good return for their work: If one falls down, his friend can help him up. But pity the man who falls and has no one to help him up! Also, if two lie down together, they will keep warm. But how can one keep warm alone? Though one may be overpowered, two can defend themselves. A cord of three strands is not quickly broken."

The life of Christ must express itself in us both individually and corporately. God holds each person responsible for his or her own spiritual walk. He also intends for us to function in the company of others. The prayer of two has special power and blessing (Matthew 18:19-20). One life sharpens another (Proverbs 27:17).

Sometimes even a brief encounter with someone who is alive in Christ can fan a diminished flame. The benefit may even come in the form of a helpful book.

10. Have I asked if God is trying to teach me something?

Have you considered that nothing may be wrong, but that everything may be right? God led Jesus into the desert for 40 days of testing. Moses spent 40 years in desert obscurity as part of God's training program for Israel. David fled from crevice to cave in those 12 years on the lam in the wilderness.

The desert can be part of God's plan to teach, train, and refine us for greater fruitfulness. In the parched place, we remember that man does not live by bread alone, but by every word that comes from the mouth of God (Deuteronomy 8:3). Even though we miss the sense of His nearness, we realize that it is better to wait for Him in the desert than to seek someone or something else by the pools. Like Peter, we say, "Lord, to whom shall we go? You have the words of eternal life" (John 6:68).

Above all, in the desert place we must remember that without faith it is impossible to please Him. He rewards those who diligently seek Him. When we find ourselves in the arid land, we can look to Him with confidence to show us if our need is to confess and forsake some sin, to rethink our motivations, to recover something of first love, or to merely relax in the assurance that even this disconcerting dryness is part of His hand of training and blessing.

Background Scripture: Psalm 139:23-24; Luke 8:14; Revelation 2:5a

Jean Fleming and her husband have ministered for about 30 years with the Navigators, an organization known for helping believers develop a deeper relationship with Christ. Jean is the mother of three grown children and the author of two books: *A Mother's Heart* (NavPress) and *Finding Focus in a Whirlwind World* (Roper Press).

2

After the Divorce

by Lynn Hallimore

I PERCHED on a flat gray rock and let the wispy mist of Yosemite's thundering waterfall cool my face. The strenuous hike that wound beneath the shadow of El Capitan and ushered me into wooded beauty proved worth the effort. For with each weary step, I left my trials further behind.

I would have never attempted such an excursion on my own. But a husband and wife from church planned and led the Yosemite trip for our church's single adult group. I'm glad they did. For in that gorgeous setting of flowered meadows, God convinced me that if He could direct a crashing waterfall, He could show me how to face my unknown future and regain my enthusiasm for living.

The pain that accompanied my divorce had drained my spiritual zeal. Gone, too, were some of my most cherished dreams of building the ideal family. My soul became so parched I doubted God could ever use me again.

I needed a guiding voice to help me find God's direction for my life. My life was a mess, and I felt alone and imprisoned in my grief.

But Psalm 68:6a says, "God sets the lonely in families, he leads forth the prisoners with singing."

That's just what God did through my church family.

How My Church Helped

1. Encouragement. I found coping with a broken heart was like riding a bike with nearly flat tires. It takes twice as much effort to pick up any speed. That's why I so appreciated the cards and friendly phone calls:

"Hi! Just checking to see how it's going."

"I want you to know we love you and Jessica."

"How did work go today?"

"What would you like me to include in my prayer time?"

"I found a Scripture verse I thought you might enjoy."

2. Child care. Once I realized I had to go back to working outside the home, I started to worry about child care for my 14-month-old daughter. I had always wanted to stay home and raise my own children. Now my circumstances made this impossible.

A woman from church learned I was looking for a Christian to care for my daughter. She referred me to her neighbor and friend, Barbara.

I struggled with leaving Jessica there. But Barbara found ways to make it a little bit easier. At the end of the day, she took time to tell me about their activities: baking cookies (we got a plateful to take home), or a walk in the park (Jessica presented me with a rumpled bouquet she had picked), or shopping.

Every now and then, Barbara took pictures of Jessica, capturing daily life on film for me. I enjoyed seeing pictures of my little girl helping wash the car while wheeling around in her walker. Barbara gave me the pictures for Jessica's photo album.

This lady was committed to taking good care of my favorite little girl in the world. She acted like watching Jessica was a privilege.

3. Meals together. In July, my refrigerator broke down for the second time in two weeks, spoiling a week's groceries. This was after Jessica had kept me up two nights in a row. At work I received a phone call. "Lynn, would you have dinner with us?" What welcome words from some church friends.

I discovered Sundays can be hard for divorced people. Watching happy and whole families leave the church parking lot sometimes makes it hard to go home to a quiet house. So the single adults organized potlucks at individuals' homes after the church services.

One of the worst things about divorce is that it robs you of your family niche, your place of belonging. On Wednesday evenings, our entire church ate together in the church fellowship hall. I loved to sit with Jessica at a full table of chattering, happy people. Adopted aunts, uncles, grandmas, and grandpas would tease and joke.

Holidays made me feel vulnerable too. Especially all the "firsts." My first Christmas alone, first Mother's Day, first birthday. But some of those firsts turned into the most memorable. I believe Jessica got four Christmas stockings that year.

4. Manual labor. Sometimes I needed help with things I found impossible to do myself. When the landlord raised the rent on my duplex, I was forced to move to something more affordable. Three men from the young marrieds' class moved Jessica and me to our new apartment. I couldn't have moved my furniture without their muscle. Their good-natured availability eased my throbbing pride.

A mechanic who attended our church checked out my car after a garage had changed the thermostat three times. The car still overheated. My Christian friend pinpointed the problem and fixed it.

5. Anonymous gifts of money. Although my ex-husband did not regularly help with child support, God provided for Jessica and me through my jobs as a medical assistant and a weekend cleaning person in an office. However, malfunctioning appliances or car trouble continually created extra expenses. My paycheck covered rent, food, and child care—but not much else.

On those rare occasions, when everything blitzed at once, we didn't have money for the simple pleasures of life. One of those times I was informed that an anonymous envelope waited for me in the church office. I opened it to find enough money for a trip to the zoo and lunch at McDonald's.

Such things are not terribly expensive, but when you're broke, an extra few dollars can seem like a small fortune. With just a few dollars we could buy Jessica new lace socks for dress up and a bottle of bubbles, or a new storybook and a small inflatable wading pool, or breakfast at a restaurant. (At one restaurant children ate for 99 cents. Jessica could finish only half the breakfast. I ate the other half, plus a short stack of pancakes and a cup of coffee.)

Financial help came in other forms as well. Retired senior adults in our church grew magnificent gardens, and they shared their fresh fruit and vegetables with us. Every contribution helped ease our budget.

6. Retreats paid in full. My church has a scholarship fund to send single adults on weekend retreats. The idea is to offer a break for single parents, to renew their perspective and strength. Some individual families provided this same ministry by offering a free weekend stay at the family cabin.

Once, during a particularly bleak time, my friend Colleen arranged a weekend for just the two of us. Her husband stayed home and watched the kids.

Colleen and I toured the back roads of gold country, enjoying the running streams and timbered mountains around the small towns of Jackson, Sonora, and Calaveras. There were antique shops to visit, trails to walk, and beautiful vistas to admire—the kind that allow claustrophobics fantastic release. No responsibilities. No problems. No decisions.

I couldn't understand why Colleen kept cracking jokes and acting . . . well . . . kind of goofy. She didn't explain until we laughed so much we cried. "Oh, Lynn! It's so good to hear you laugh. I don't believe I've heard you laugh in months, and I've missed your laughter."

7. Accepting me as divorced, but Christian. My church family refused to let me consider myself as no longer useful in ministry. Instead, they assured me, "Your life isn't over. God has a purpose for you. We need you. You belong here."

Although I hadn't taught Sunday School for the last six months, I was scheduled to teach a fall class of high school girls. Since I knew my church didn't ask divorced people to serve as deacon, I assumed they wouldn't want a divorced person in a teaching position either. I was shocked when my Sunday School director said, "You can't quit teaching."

"But what about my life's example?" I asked her. "What kind of impact will it have on the kids? What's good about it? Where's the Christian victory?"

"Lynn," she said, "you have the perfect opportunity to exemplify living out the Christian walk despite great difficulty. Do you think all these kids come from perfect families? You can show them how to not give up your relationship with God while enduring difficulties—a tool they can use throughout life."

I wasn't convinced.

"Why don't you discuss this with Pastor?" she suggested.

Pastor assured me, "Lynn, God doesn't hold you accountable for your husband's choices in life. I think you should teach your girls and love them with all the love God can give you."

I believe I floated out of his office.

This was the first time since the divorce that I considered my situation as something other than a detriment. I could tell my girls about how my homelife forced me to depend completely on God. And I could tell them how my eyes would grow wide as I watched Him provide time after time.

During a class slumber party, giggling teenage girls covered my living room floor with wall-to-wall sleeping bags. I felt like a proud mother hen in a snug flannel nest. Together we sang songs and celebrated the joy God brings to living.

At first, I found church programs such as "How to Overcome Discouragement" or "How to Survive Divorce" helpful for my own personal growth. But then I reached the point where I just wanted to be accepted as normal. I wanted people to see me the way Jesus did, as a vessel ready for use, cleansed by His blood. No longer grieving, I chose to mesh back into the church body and benefit from courses ranging from discipleship to Bible book studies.

When It Was My Turn to Help

Often, I dreamed of being able to pay back the kindnesses shown to me. I had been overwhelmed with the love of God I received from fellow Christians. Yet, when it came time for God to love someone through me, I realized "pay back" isn't the way the Body of Christ works.

Instead of urging me to return the favors of those who had helped me, the Holy Spirit prompted me to help others in need. This way, His love and kindness could work like a chain reaction that never stops.

Christians are not indebted to one another. They are indebted to Christ. Colossians 3:17 says, "And whatever you do, whether in word or deed, do it all in the name of the Lord Jesus, giving thanks to God the Father through him."

An unexpected Christmas bonus from my boss allowed me the opportunity to encourage another single mother at our church. This woman had fled her physically abusive husband, taking only one suitcase and her preschool son. Her dad and mom lived out of state. Distance and finances kept her from going home for the holiday.

When Jessica and I delivered our gaily wrapped presents, there wasn't a tree to place them under. The empty living room echoed without furniture. Only a double mattress lay on the bedroom floor. The young mother welcomed our gifts.

"This is such an answer to prayer!" she said. "I wanted my boy to have something special for Christmas, and God provided." Her shining brown eyes looked as if they had just witnessed a miracle. My mother's heart understood.

After we left that day, I couldn't decide which was more thrilling: sensing God reaching out and loving me through another Christian, or feeling His inner prompting to help someone else. Through this simple act of giving came a renewed passion for living.

When we allow others to help us, or when we help them, we push past the boundaries of our own pride and self-sufficiency. Complete with goose bumps, we watch God's extraordinary love and power begin its work that invigorates, stimulates, and provides spiritual renewal.

Background Scripture: Psalm 68:4-10; Colossians 3:17; James 2:14-17

Lynn Hallimore has remarried and is a homemaker and a part-time writer and medical assistant in El Dorado Hills, Calif.

3

She's My Enemy

by Barbara Tetlow Beevers

"THEN THERE'S MISS SIMMONS." Betsy almost hissed as she pronounced the initial *s*.

"Don't take her for English 101. She's awful. I hate . . . no, I don't hate her, because Christians aren't supposed to hate people." She frowned, and then a sheepish smile of relief flashed across her pretty face. "I guess I just love her as an enemy!"

I've always remembered Betsy's puzzled expression and that somewhat smug remark. Was she really content to gloss over the conflict between her real feelings and what she thought Christians *should* feel?

I, too, have wondered what it means to love an enemy. Surely it's not just a polite, Christian way of expressing dislike. But if I love someone, doesn't that make the person a friend and not an enemy? What is an enemy, anyway? Is it someone I dislike? Is it someone who opposes or hates me?

These questions were only academic until I encountered prejudice as a white, blue-eyed American in an Asian country. I knew some Asians consider Americans bossy and proud. Yet I was surprised when a translator resented my asking why he had used one word instead of another. I wanted to better understand those two words, but he perceived my question as criticism.

I suspected he was prejudging me. Maybe he considers me his enemy, I thought, but I do not dislike him.

While he looked on me as an adversary before he even knew me, I saw him as a potential friend. Even if he hated me, I wouldn't hate him. Perhaps this was the meaning of loving an enemy.

Once I had guessed the reason for his hostility, I looked for ways to turn my "enemy" into a friend. Scripture says we are to treat our enemies in this way: we are to pray for them, bless them, and do good to them.

As I sought chances to talk to him, I was careful not to seem critical. When I asked for his advice, I made sure my words were clearly a request for his help. I didn't say, "Why did you . . . ?" or worse yet, "Why didn't you . . . ?" Instead, I asked, "What did you think about this?" or "Which is better?"

It worked! Soon we were working together in harmony. That's because I had loved him when he considered me his enemy, and now we were friends.

The Woman Who Refused to Reconcile

The next time I had a conflict, my attempts at reconciliation didn't work. My husband and I had been welcomed into the fellowship of a small church. For many months we enjoyed rather ideal relationships there. But suddenly, a woman who at first had been very friendly turned against me with criticism and faultfinding. I went to her and tried to explain that I had not done the things she accused me of. Certainly I had not meant to hurt her feelings.

She didn't believe me. She persisted in thinking I had wronged her. It seemed as if she *wanted* to find faults in me to complain about.

Eventually I realized this was not a misunderstanding

I could clear up, as I had with my Asian friend.

Once, fortified with hours of prayer and Bible study, I phoned her. "The Sunday School lesson was about reconciliation. Could we get together and talk about it?" Not only did she turn down my suggestion, but weeks later, when I greeted her after church, she said in a mocking tone, "How are you doing in your reconciliation efforts?"

It was hard to admit that her hatred was against me personally. I tend to like everybody, and I try to please. Not being able to win her over has been a major disappointment. But after trying for three years, I'm ready to admit I have an enemy.

Webster's New Collegiate Dictionary says an enemy is "one hostile to another; one who seeks the overthrow or failure of that to which he is opposed." So an enemy is not just someone I dislike. *My* feelings are not the determining factor. *Hers* are. And her feelings are not simple dislike, but hatred strong enough to seek my downfall. That's the kind of person Jesus tells us to love.

How Do You Love an Enemy?

How can I obey Jesus' command to love her? So far, I have found four ways.

1. I forgive her unconditionally and repeatedly. I used to think that repentance was necessary on the part of the wrongdoer before I was obligated to forgive. But in studying Scripture, I have noticed that neither the murderers of Jesus nor of Stephen expressed any repentance, and yet both Jesus and Stephen asked God to forgive them.

I have truthfully been able to say that I forgive this woman. But it hasn't been a once-and-for-all kind of forgiveness. Often another person will hear what my enemy has said or done, and then sympathize or urge me to seek reconciliation. Each time the subject comes up, my disappointment and hurt come back, and I must deal with my feelings all over again. I've asked God to help me with my emotions, and He has—over and over again.

Many times she has seemed to have a change of heart, and I have thought my prayers were answered. She smiles or speaks a pleasant word to me, and I respond eagerly, only to have her deliver a barb that smarts for days. Once she said, "I was in this church before you came, and I'll be here after you've gone." I felt like a cowboy in a Western movie to whom the sheriff has just snarled, "I'll ride you out of town."

But it's not just the past I have to deal with. Today I am more afraid of what she *will* do than angry about what she *has* done. Sometimes I see her at the shopping center, and I feel a stab of apprehension. What will she say? How will I respond? I have learned that forgiveness may not come easily, but it must come *repeatedly.*

2. I look to Scripture for God's evaluation of the situation and for comfort. It is possible that some of her criticisms are true. When she interrupted a Bible study by saying, "How can you teach when you don't love people?" I was speechless with shock.

Others defended me, but I went home and asked the Lord if what she had said was true. The Lord reassured me that her words were not His vehicle of correction this time as I read the words of Isaiah, "If anyone does attack you, it will not be my doing" (54:15*a*).

God's Word has been like salve on my wounds. Words I had seen but not felt before have come alive with meaning. I know more of what the prophets felt when they were rejected, how Jesus felt when He was betrayed. And I have experienced God's comfort.

3. I take action. The first action is prayer. "Pray for those who persecute you" (Matthew 5:44*b*). I have found it fairly easy to pray for my enemy because it bothers me so much to *have* an enemy. I ask the Lord to bring her to repentance for the anger and bitterness she shows to others but does not admit to herself. I pray, "Search me, O God, and know my heart . . . See if there is any offensive way in me" (Psalm 139:23-24). I pray this for her as well as for myself. I picture her receiving refreshment from the Lord as a result of repentance (Acts 3:19). Again and again I ask God for the power to love her and the power to forgive her.

Romans 12:14-21 has guided me through this whole process. Verses 14 and 17 have kept me from responding to her cutting remarks with barbs of my own: "Bless those who persecute you; bless and do not curse. . . . Do not repay anyone evil for evil."

The qualifying clauses in verse 18, "If it is possible, as far as it depends on you," have helped me recognize that sometimes it is not possible to "live at peace with everyone" and that a solution is not entirely dependent on me. This has kept me from false guilt.

I also ask God to reveal specific ways I can act toward her. Verse 20 says: "If your enemy is hungry, feed him; if he is thirsty, give him something to drink." My enemy is neither hungry nor thirsty; in material things she is rich. But she is hungry for praise. So I search for opportunities to give her a sincere compliment.

Luke 6:35 also says to look for ways to do good and be kind. I'm not often tempted to be unkind or to hurt her; I just want to avoid her. Still, Jesus says to take the initiative in approaching her. Do good. Be kind.

I have found two pitfalls in my attempts to do good to my enemy. I still want to win her over, so I may focus too much attention on her and neglect others who are open to my friendship and teaching. Perhaps the time will come when she will need my help. But in the meantime, I've decided to follow some good advice from a friend. "Don't let criticism put you in a defensive mode," she said. "Keep on getting your plans from the Lord." That means I don't let my enemy define my ministry or even let her criticisms control my schedule.

The other pitfall is the pain I feel. I want to do good to her, but when I see her, my guard goes up. How can I minister to someone who hurts me? My own hurt blinds and deafens me to her crying need. It's like trying to pet and comfort a porcupine. Each time I reach out, I get another bleeding wound.

I find comfort in knowing that Jesus experienced this guardedness too. "Jesus would not entrust himself to them . . . for he knew what was in a man" (John 2:24-25). Yet Jesus, and Stephen too, at the time of death, were able to break through preoccupation with their own pain. They didn't think only of how much the nails or the stones hurt, but of their enemies' need for forgiveness. I don't know if the words "Father, forgive them" made any impression on those enemies, but they have revealed the heart of God to many of us since.

4. Finally, I refuse to hate her or wish her ill. Although I cannot escape having an enemy, I am determined not to *be* an enemy. Receiving hatred has been hard. But with God's help I can keep it from settling in my heart.

Sometimes the psalmists prayed that calamity would fall on their enemies. I guess that shows how human they were. But it wasn't Jesus' style, and I don't want it to be mine.

The world will not see the Father's unconditional love for them unless we Christians model it. Whether it's a sister or a son who is opposing me, I want to keep reaching out, to keep hoping for reconciliation. But even if reconciliation never comes, I can win a different kind of victory. I can obey my Lord and honor Jesus' name by loving my enemy.

Background Scripture: Matthew 5:43-47; Romans 12:14-21

Barbara Tetlow Beevers leads discipleship training in a church her husband pastors in Savage, Md. Before that they were missionaries to Indonesia.

4

It's a Busy Life

by Dean Nelson

THE FIRST FEW MONTHS of this year were busy for my family—and I know what you're thinking: Everybody's busy, pal, so spare us the list of all the stuff you're doing. We're doing stuff too. You just get to write about it, and, frankly, it sounds like you're bragging. So give it a rest, Mr. Phone-in-the-Car.

But you're wrong. I don't have a phone in my car. I barely have a floor in there now (I do a great Flintstones impression), so a phone would look a little silly. Also, I know you're busy. In fact, I'm presuming you're so busy that you have the same kind of trouble I do in finding time for spiritual things.

So, back to my busy months. My two children are under five, my wife is an accountant (remember April 15 and the months leading up to it?), I had two book deadlines looming near, I was preparing for a trip to Central America on a writing assignment, and I was trying to recover from knee surgery performed at the beginning of the year. That's when I got a call from the *New York Times* asking me to do a story for them on the merger of two major newspapers in San Diego.

"Sure," I said to the editor from the *Times*. "By Thursday this week would be no problem."

There are certain editors and publications a writer never turns down. Writers live in fear that the editors may never call again. It's a lot like dating, from what I'm told.

The first couple of days after the *Times* called, I did a lot of interviewing and preparing for that story. The night before it was due, I started my prewriting ritual: I got out a bag of coffee beans, assembled the grinder, and prepared the coffeepot. Methodically I poured the beans into the grinder and switched it on. Immediately I could smell the marvelous aroma of freshly ground Colombian beans filling the kitchen. I stood with my hands on the counter on either side of the grinder, head toward the ceiling, and inhaled the fumes as if they were from a fine perfume. But something didn't sound right after a couple of seconds. I looked down and saw that I hadn't inserted the container to catch the newly ground beans. The grinder was spewing them all over my pink sweater and throughout the kitchen.

In a flash I made an appliance switch—from coffee grinder to hand-vac. I dust-busted the counter, the stove, the floor, my sweater, my slacks, shoes, and socks. I tried to get all the bean chunks, but I missed plenty. For weeks it seemed like every time we moved a canister or something in that part of the house, it would look like there had been a convention of mice, if you catch my meaning.

I learned something in those hectic months. When our days are filled with doing things—even good things—we can lose our focus and do dumb stuff like I did with the coffee grinder. Worse, we can treat each other like we treat some of those appliances—useful for the moment, then no longer necessary. We can do that with the ones we love most, like our spouses and children. I know what I'm talking about here.

It is possible to do too many good things. It's possible that, in the middle of doing things like evangelism, Sunday

School teaching, and choir, along with holding down a job and trying to raise kids, we're drying up inside. Then we wonder why we're so tired and why we feel so frustrated or hollow despite our involvements.

The answer isn't as easy as having longer devotional time with the Lord. There are some days, because of family, career, civic, and other obligations, I simply don't have time to read God's Word and have a lively dialogue with Him. I interviewed Mrs. Louise Robinson Chapman, a retired missionary and former president of the missionary society for the Church of the Nazarene, for an article I was doing about her 100th birthday. She was complaining that her pastor said everyone should spend five minutes a day in prayer.

"If I spent only five minutes a day in prayer, I'd freeze to death," she said. I've seen her prayer list. It's huge. I felt shamed that mine consisted of scraps of paper scattered on my dresser, and that I rarely got around to them. There are days when I *don't* spend five minutes a day, and Mrs. Chapman was right—I feel like I'm freezing to death on the inside.

A Day in the Life of Jesus

Perhaps those of us who think we're busy need to pay attention to a day in the life of Jesus, as recorded in Mark 1:21-35.

They came to Capernaum, and on the Sabbath he went to synagogue and began to teach. The people were astounded at his teaching, for, unlike the doctors of the law, he taught with a note of authority. Now there was a man in the synagogue possessed by an unclean spirit. He shrieked: "What do you want with us, Jesus of Nazareth? Have you come to destroy us? I know who you are—the Holy One of God." Jesus re-

buked him: "Be silent," he said, "and come out of him."
And the unclean spirit threw the man into convulsions
and with a loud cry left him. They were all dumb-
founded and began to ask one another, "What is this? A
new kind of teaching! He speaks with authority. When
he gives orders, even the unclean spirits submit." The
news spread rapidly, and he was soon spoken of all
over the district of Galilee *(New English Bible)*.

That was just the morning. Maybe they broke for
lunch, but here's how they spent the afternoon.

"On leaving the synagogue they went straight to the
house of Simon and Andrew; and James and John went
with them. Simon's mother-in-law was ill in bed with
fever. They told him about her at once. He came forward,
took her by the hand, and helped her to her feet. The fever
left her and she waited upon them."

But they were a long ways from being done for the
day.

"That evening after sunset they brought to him all
who were ill or possessed by devils; and the whole town
was there, gathered at the door. He healed many who suf-
fered from various diseases, and drove out many devils."

Pretty big day. It was made possible, though, because
of the kind of thing that happened the next morning, as
shown in verse 35.

"Very early next morning he got up and went out. He
went away to a lonely spot and remained there in prayer."

In that verse is the blueprint for what it takes to keep a
spiritual vitality in a busy life—moments stolen away for
silence, reflection, solitude, and prayer. Sometimes the moments can be worked into the routine. Sometimes not.
Sometimes they occur as a result of divine accidents, as I
believe occurred in my case with my car. The radio went
out. I was driving to Los Angeles from San Diego, and the

dumb thing just quit. I'm a news junkie, and I *need* that radio to tell me what's going on around the world.

I pulled the car off on the shoulder of the road and crawled as far behind my dashboard as I could to see if a wire had just broken loose. No luck. I was doomed to silence. But within a half hour of not hearing about world hot spots, gang shootings, and unbalanced budgets, something strange happened. I started thinking about people. I found myself praying for them, remembering things they had said they were going through. There I was, driving 65 miles per hour on Interstate 15, talking and listening to God. I even hummed a couple of praise songs I hadn't thought of in years.

Could it be that God was using this time when I was finally a captive audience? I hoped so. This drive was hardly what you'd call getting out early in the morning to a lonely spot for prayer, but it was doing the job.

The Value of Solitude

Author Henri Nouwen, in his book *Out of Solitude*, says Jesus shows us that right in the middle of involvement must be withdrawal, in the middle of action must be contemplation, in the middle of togetherness must be solitude, in the middle of ministry must be silence. There must be the latter part of each phrase, or the former won't be around very long.

A recent *Los Angeles Times* story also told of the value of solitude. A psychotherapist in the story said solitude helps a person make rational decisions. "You're not as inclined to be impulsive; you're not as inclined to be foolish in doing things that are self-destructive or harmful to other people," he said. He added that those interested in developing a spiritual life have to do so, in part, in solitude.

In our culture of constant distraction, this is not an

easy concept. Being quiet doesn't come naturally to us anymore. Yet it is in the quiet times that we pray and hear deeply, which is what gives us our spiritual strength. Sociologist George Barna, in his book *The Power of Vision*, wrote that leaders of American churches generally feel successful only when they are active. "God, however, seems to speak most clearly to Christian leaders when they are inactive; that is, when they have made a conscious effort to allow Him to lead the conversation and to impart wisdom in His own way, in His own timing."

The quiet moments can come during times other than driving too. A woman in my Sunday School class said her time for praying and listening is when she irons clothes. The temptation is to turn on the TV, she said, but when it is just her, doing the repetitious act, dialogue with God occurs.

It happens for me when I work in my yard. The repetitious act of pulling weeds is boring and makes my back sore. But God breaks through during those times. Stuff gets sorted out. Gerard Reed, chaplain at Point Loma Nazarene College, says he prays when he runs. It's not Gethsemane, but it works.

While I was working on my Ph.D., we as a family lived in the rural town of Athens, Ohio, home of Ohio University. Because of the surrounding Appalachian Mountains, television signals were difficult to get; so if you wanted to watch TV, you had to get cable. We were living on school loans, so it was obvious to us that we'd need to do without it for two years. I quit studying at around 10:00 each night, and my wife and I would sit on the front porch for a while. Sometimes we said a lot to each other to catch up on the day. Sometimes we didn't say a word. It was one of the most crucial parts in the day, because it was a chance to clear out the distractions and just be. If I were king, I would proclaim that every family had to do without television for two years. It would change a lot of things.

There is one more thing I believe should be turned off occasionally if a person is going to experience some quiet in the day or night. The telephone. We have an on/off switch on ours for this very reason. During dinner it's off. During important family discussions it's off. During rare times of family devotions it's off. There is no law that says it must be picked up when it rings. It's not a crying baby. But you can be if you feel obligated to answer it all the time.

How I Preserve My Spiritual Vitality

As Nouwen points out, solitude makes community possible. And community is one of the crucial elements in retaining a spiritual life. For some people the community experience occurs at church, Sunday School, Bible study, care groups, or other similar gatherings.

For me it is a group I meet with for breakfast once a week. There are four of us and, with the exception of one member, we have met this way for eight years. We act as a support group, and we intercede for each other. We go through books together and discuss them. We share our joys and hurts. And we know that, during the week, we are praying for each other. Having that group helps keep life in perspective for me.

There are two other ways I have found helpful in retaining vitality. And they don't demand huge hunks of time. The first one is teaching a Sunday School class. Even if it is for little kids, it forces grown-ups like me into the Word and makes us confront what we think about what we read. Applying the Scripture to daily life is something we don't necessarily do unless we are forced to.

The second one is praying with my kids. Before they

go to bed, we often talk about what we should be praying for. Some of the most eloquent prayers I've heard have come from my five-year-old when he was praying for his cousin who had been in a serious car accident, and for her brother and sister so they wouldn't be too lonely without her. He thinks of things that have never crossed my mind, and it makes me pray too. Sometimes I feel as if I am eavesdropping on a very holy moment between him and God. It's energizing.

These four areas: solitude, community, organizing thoughts about the Word, and praying as a family are what keep me from spraying coffee grounds all over the house most of the time.

This is not a prescription for avoiding spiritual burn-out. It's just a glimpse of some practices that help me.

I'm overcommitted, I admit it. I think most of us are. But let's not commit ourselves right out of an abundant relationship with Christ. I'm hungry for more of the *abundant* life. But what I get is more of the *busy* life.

Can both occur? As I read the first chapter of Mark, I can say, with relief, that the answer is yes.

Background Scripture: Mark 1:21-35

Dean Nelson teaches journalism at Point Loma Nazarene College, San Diego, and is a contributor to the *New York Times* and the *Boston Globe*.

5

If You Want to Grow Up,
Become a Child

by Michael Card

IT'S 4:17 A.M. Our three-year-old is rolling around at the foot of our waterbed. The salesman went to great lengths to convince us this was a "waveless" mattress, but Katie is able nonetheless to make waves. So I am gently being rocked awake.

I look down at her. She is smiling. Is she afraid because she has awakened me? No. She is filled with reckless confidence and so trusts her dad not to wallop her. She also knows that if I did, she would cry and wake up everyone else in the house. So she smiles fearlessly.

Her gown is on backward. It makes more sense to her that way, and I must confess, it does to me too. The buttons are now on the front where she can get at them, and the lace that used to adorn the front is on the back, which makes for a much more impressive exit.

She rolls around giggling as I close my eyes. But she wanders up to my face and pats it to see if I'm still awake. I try to protect myself from being kicked in places I'd rather not be kicked, but to no avail.

The worst thing Katie could do now is to reach over

and tickle her little brother, Will. So that of course is what she does. He cries; I get up and change a wet diaper.

In the midst of this seemingly miserable morning the Lord awakens something in me and invites me to listen. He is speaking to me through my children. For some time now I've been teaching others about becoming a child again. And now, this morning, the Lord begins to teach me in a deeper way what I've been trying to teach others.

I haven't been able to sleep much this night, worrying about a hometown concert the next day, and thinking about regrets in my life. Sometimes it seems like I was born to worry.

My little girl, like her dad, couldn't sleep either. But her response? To roll around and play, to smile, and to tickle her little brother awake so that he can join in the fun. Is she concerned about past failures? Is she worried about the long, hard life that lies before her? No. For her, the passion of the present moment is all there is. She invites me to join her there. And in my heart of hearts, I long to come.

Jesus said, "I tell you the truth, unless you change and become like little children, you will never enter the kingdom of heaven" (Matthew 18:3). What does Jesus mean by this?

The more I read the Bible and the more I pour my life into my children, the more I become convinced that becoming childlike represents the same transformation as becoming Christlike. Why else could Jesus make this a condition for entering the kingdom of heaven?

A close look at the Gospels reveals Jesus himself, in many ways, lived the life of a child. He lived in simplicity, naïveté, and He had a passion for the present moment, along with a reckless confidence.

The Simplicity of Jesus

Children live simple lives. They eat, sleep, and play.

As long as their basic needs are met, they are usually happy.

Jesus of Nazareth showed that same simplicity. When His disciples asked Him to teach them to pray, the Master recited a simple prayer. "Our Father," He began. Then He went on to praise, to ask for food for the day, forgiveness, and the strength to forgive. Any child can pray this prayer and understand it.

To embrace simplicity, Jesus had to reject much of the busyness of the world—and so do we. "You are worried and upset about many things," Jesus gently told Martha, who was busy preparing a meal. "But only one thing is needed. Mary has chosen what is better" (Luke 10:41-42). In that moment, Mary was sitting at Jesus' feet in childlike simplicity, listening.

We can still make the choice Martha made, and drive ourselves and everyone around to busyness. There is always the kitchen, the office, the chores of the world. But there is also that place Jesus has reserved for us at His feet, to listen, to learn, and to find enjoyment in His presence.

A Lesson in Naïveté

Katie asks innocent questions and naively believes anything I tell her. Her confidence lies, not in the believability of my answers (they often seem unbelievable to her, I'm certain), but in the faith she has in the one who gives her the answers. Because I am her father, she believes what I say.

Like a child, Jesus was sometimes perceived as being painfully naive. "Doesn't he know what kind of woman is touching him?" the Pharisees once asked, as if Jesus didn't know what all the makeup and provocative clothing meant. "It would take eight months' wages to feed this crowd!" the disciples once gasped. What a naive proposition it seemed Jesus was making.

Jesus' childlike naïveté should become the pattern for our own lives. We need to accept everything our Father tells us, no matter how much it violates the norm and even our own sense of reason. Paul tells us in 1 Corinthians 13:7 that love is trust, which believes all things. Isn't that, after all, the definition of naïveté?

Passion for the Present Moment

When my children are at play, their game is all that exists for them. The concept that they must be somewhere by a certain time, like church, is lost on them. They are absorbed in the present moment, and for them that really is all there is.

Jesus had the same quality of allowing himself to become totally absorbed in the present moment. Though the most important agenda on earth awaited Him, He lavished attention on even the most seemingly unimportant person. Anyone who had His attention was the most important person in the world. Jesus had a passion for the present.

Two forces drain the life from the present moment: guilt drags us into the past, and fear pulls us into the future. But if we belong to Christ, what do fear or guilt have to do with us? Our guilt is gone, washed away by His blood. And fear? If we need not be afraid of Jesus, we need not be afraid of anything.

Jesus invites us into the moment, where His children dwell, to live guiltless and fearless in His presence.

Reckless Confidence in the Father

The source of Katie's reckless confidence on the waterbed was the relationship she has with her father. She knows that her mother and I are on her side. Even when she is wrong, especially when she is wrong, we are on her side. Our love is not based on her obedience. She is our child, and that is that.

Because she knows this, she lives recklessly, on the edge. If there has to be some disciplining, she knows that afterward there will be hugs and kisses.

Jesus never needed discipline from the Father. Yet He lived with reckless confidence. So confident was Jesus in His relationship with God that He called Him by a name no one in the history of religion had ever dared call God. Others (notably the Pharisees) had used the name "Father" in talking to God. But Jesus called Him *Abba.*

Let no one clothe that name with theological sophistication. It is not a sophisticated word. *Abba,* quite simply, is baby talk. Our children stammer "papa" from the Latin *pater,* for father. Hebrew babies first stutter the name *Abba* from the Hebrew word *ab,* which also means father.

Jesus chose this tender term for the God of the universe. Jesus called Him by that name, I believe, because Jesus lived as a child before God, His Father. He invites you and me to come to the Father just as intimately.

Through the Holy Spirit we, too, can call our God *Abba.* "Because you are sons, God sent the Spirit of his Son into our hearts, the Spirit who calls out, '*Abba,* Father'" (Galatians 4:6).

It is our right. "To all who received him, to those who believed in his name, he gave the right to become children of God" (John 1:12).

"'Let the little children come to me, and do not hinder them, for the kingdom of God belongs to such as these. I tell you the truth, anyone who will not receive the kingdom of God like a little child will never enter it.' And he took the children in his arms, put his hands on them and blessed them" (Mark 10:14b-16).

This is the call of Jesus to become a child again. Only in accepting this invitation can we hope to "grow up" in Him.

May we listen as He invites us to live with a passion little known and seldom seen in this flat, gray, and fallen world. For in the Kingdom it will be a little child who will lead the calf and the lion (Isaiah 11:6). It could *only* be a little child, since Jesus tells us there will be no other sort of person there.

Background Scripture: Matthew 18:1-4; Mark 10:13-16; Luke 10:38-42

Michael Card is a singer and songwriter whose compositions include "El Shaddai," "Celebrate the Child," and "Immanuel." He is the author of *Immanuel: Reflections on the Life of Christ* (Thomas Nelson) and *Sleep Sound in Jesus* (Harvest House).

6

Healing for Perfectionism, the Counterfeit Holiness

by David A. Seamands

THERE IS A BIG DIFFERENCE between true Christian perfection and perfectionism. Though at first glance they may look alike, there is a great gulf between the two.

Perfectionism is a counterfeit for Christian perfection, holiness, sanctification, or the Spirit-filled life. Instead of making us holy persons—that is, whole persons in Christ —perfectionism leaves us spiritual Pharisees and emotional neurotics.

You think I'm exaggerating? You think this is some newfangled discovery by psychologists or the pastor? I want to assure you that throughout the centuries, sensitive pastors observed these kinds of suffering Christians and were deeply concerned.

John Fletcher, a contemporary of John Wesley in the 1700s, described certain of his parishioners:

> Some bind heavy burdens on themselves of their own making and when they cannot bear them, they are tormented in their consciences with imaginary guilt. Others go distracted through groundless fears of having committed the unpardonable sin. In a word,

do we not see hundreds who, when they have reason to think well of their state, instead think there is no hope for them whatever?

The circuit-riding pastor and founder of Methodism, John Wesley, recorded it this way:

> Sometimes this excellent quality, tenderness of conscience, is carried to an extreme. We find some who fear where no fear is, who are continually condemning themselves without cause, imagining something to be sinful where Scripture nowhere condemns it.

One ancient minister actually wrote a book about perfectionism, called *The Spiritual Treatment of Sufferers from Nerves and Scruples.* An amazingly accurate title.

The Symptoms

Perfectionism is the most disturbing emotional problem among evangelical Christians. It walks into my office more often than any other Christian hang-up.

What is perfectionism? Since it is a lot easier to describe than to define, I want you to see some of its symptoms.

1. Tyranny of the oughts. Its chief characteristic is a constant, overall feeling of never doing well enough or being good enough. This feeling permeates all of life but especially affects our spiritual lives. Psychologist Karen Horney's classic phrase describes it perfectly: "The tyranny of the *oughts.*"

Here is its typical statement: "I ought to do better."

All the way from preparing a meal to praying or witnessing—"I didn't do it quite well enough."

If you are living in this emotional state, the official posture is standing on tiptoe, always reaching, stretching, trying, but never quite making it.

2. Self-depreciation. If you are never quite satisfied with yourself and your achievements, then the next step is quite natural: God is never really pleased with you either. He's always saying, "Come on now, you can do better than that."

So, back to the spiritual salt mines you go, with increased efforts to please yourself and an increasingly demanding God who is never quite satisfied. But you always fall short, you are inadequate, you never arrive but you must never stop trying.

3. Anxiety. The oughts and self-depreciation produce an oversensitive conscience under a giant umbrella of guilt, anxiety, and condemnation. Like a great cloud, the umbrella hangs over your head. Once in a while it lifts and the sun shines through, particularly during revivals, deeper life conferences, and retreats, when you go forward for prayer or "make a deeper surrender."

Unfortunately, the sunshine lasts about as long as it did the last time you made the same trip, went through the same process, and claimed the same blessing. Soon you fall off spiritual cloud nine with a sickening thud. Those same dreaded feelings settle in again. The general sense of divine disapproval and comprehensive condemnation return, nagging and knocking at the back door of your soul.

4. Legalism. The oversensitive conscience and comprehensive guilt of the perfectionist are usually accompanied by a legalism that rigidly overemphasizes dos and don'ts.

The perfectionist with his fragile conscience, his low self-esteem, and his almost built-in sense of guilt is very sensitive to what other people think about him. Since he cannot accept himself and is quite unsure of God's approval, he desperately needs the approval of other people. Thus he is easy prey to the opinions and evaluations of other Christians.

Every sermon gets to him. He thinks, Ah-h, maybe that's what's wrong with me. Maybe if I give this up . . . add that to my life . . . Maybe if I stop doing this or I start doing that, I will experience peace, joy, and power. Maybe then God will accept me, and I will please Him.

All the while, the dos and don'ts are piling up; they keep adding up because more and more people have to be pleased. The halo has to be adjusted for this person and readjusted for that one. So the perfectionist keeps fitting it this way and that way and, before he realizes what is happening, the halo has turned into what Paul called the "yoke of slavery" (Galatians 5:1).

The yoke was a familiar farm implement in those days, put around the necks of animals so that they could do some kind of work, like plowing. But in the Bible the yoke was also a symbol of the enslavement of a conquered people. It was something humiliating and destructive.

The good news of grace had broken into the lives of the Galatians, freeing them from that kind of spiritual yoke. The good news is that the way to God is not by the path of perfect performance. No matter how much you try, you can never *win* God's favor. Why? Because His favor, His being pleased with you, is a love-gift of His grace through Jesus Christ.

After a while, grace seemed *too good* to be true, and the Galatians began to listen to other voices in the market-place: "a different gospel," as Paul termed it (1:6). Maybe they listened to *the Jerusalem legalists,* who said even Gentile Christians had to keep all the laws God gave the Jews. Maybe they listened to *the Colossian ascetics,* who majored in giving up things in order to please God. They also majored in observing special days, new moons, and Sabbaths. They insisted on "false humility" and deliberate low self-esteem (Colossians 2:18). They stressed what Paul called *regulations*. "Do not handle! Do not taste! Do not touch!" (v. 21). Paul said they had "the appearance of wisdom in self-made religion and self-abasement," which was "of no value against fleshly indulgence" (v. 23, NASB). How accurate.

And so, the Jerusalem legalists and the Colossian ascetics produced *the Galatian diluters*. They reverted to a diluted mixture of faith and works, law and grace. Immature and sensitive believers can become neurotic perfectionists who are guilt-ridden, unhappy, and uncomfortable. They are rigid in their outlook, frigid in their lovelessness, conforming to the approval and disapproval of others. Yet, in a strange paradox, they critically judge, blame, and bind those same others.

5. Anger. But the worst is yet to come. For, you see, something terrible is beginning to happen to the perfectionist. He may not realize it, but deep in his heart a kind of anger is developing. A resentment against the oughts, against the Christian faith, against other Christians, against himself, but saddest of all, against God.

Oh, not that it's really against the true God. That's the sadness of it. The perfectionist is not against the gracious, loving, self-giving God who has come to us, who in Jesus Christ went all the way to the Cross at such cost. No, his resentment is against a caricature of a god who is never satisfied.

Sometimes his anger is recognized, and the whole wretched ought-tyranny is seen for what it is: a desperate satanic substitute for true Christian perfection. And sometimes the perfectionist can work through all this, find grace, and marvelously be set free.

6. Denial. Too often, however, the anger is not faced but denied. Because anger is considered a terrible sin, it is pushed down. And the whole mixture of bad theology, legalism, and salvation by performance becomes a frozen Niagara. This is when deep emotional problems set in. Mood changes are so great and so terrible that such a person seems to be two different people at the same time.

Under the stress and the strain of trying to live with a self he can't like, a God he can't love, and other people he can't get along with, the strain can become too much. And one of two things can happen: either there is a breakaway or a breakdown.

The *breakaway* is so sad. Much of my time is spent counseling people who used to be active Christians but who have now broken away. The breakaway just throws the whole thing over. He doesn't become an unbeliever. He believes with his head, but he can't believe with his heart. Perfectionism is impossible to live up to. He's tried so many times and it made him so miserable that he just left it behind.

Others suffer a *breakdown*. The load is too heavy to bear, and they break under the weight. That's exactly what happened to Dr. Joseph R. Cooke, professor of anthropology at the University of Washington in Seattle. A brilliant Ph.D. and well trained in biblical theology, he became a missionary teacher to Thailand. But after a few years he left the mission field a broken man. A nervous breakdown left him no longer able to preach or teach or even to read his Bible. And as he put it, "I was a burden to my wife and useless to God and to others" (*Free for the Taking*, Fleming Revell).

How did this happen? "I invented an impossible God, and I had a nervous breakdown." Oh, he believed in grace; he even taught it. But his real feelings about the god he lived with day by day didn't correspond with his teaching. His god was ungracious and unpleasable.

Can you understand why a sincere Christian who feels this way would have a total breakdown? And my years of preaching and counseling and praying with evangelical Christians lead me to believe that this disease of perfectionism is common among church people.

The Cure

There is only one cure for perfectionism: it is profound and yet as simple as the word *grace*.

In the New Testament this word has a special meaning: "freely given, undeserved, unmerited, unearnable, and unrepayable favor." God's loving acceptance of us has nothing to do with our worthiness.

Grace is the face God wears when He meets our imperfection, sin, weakness, and failure. Grace is what God is and what God does when He meets the sinful and undeserving. Grace is a pure gift, free for the taking.

The healing of perfectionism does not begin with some initial experience of grace in salvation or sanctification, and then move into a life lived by effort and perfect performance. The healing of perfectionism takes place in day-by-day believing, living, and realizing this grace relationship with a loving, caring Heavenly Father.

But that's the rub, for sometimes this cannot happen by itself. The realization of grace cannot be maintained in some people without an inner healing of the past. God's care cannot be felt without a deep, inner reprogramming of all the bad conditioning that has been put into them by parents and family and teachers and preachers and the church.

These perfectionists have been programmed to unrealistic expectations, impossible performance, conditional love, and a subtle theology of works. They can't get rid of this pattern overnight. The change requires time, process,

understanding, healing, and above all, reprogramming—
the renewal of the mind that brings transformation.

I want to tell you how it happened in one young
man's life. Don was raised in a strict evangelical home,
where everything they believed in their heads was right,
but where everything they practiced in everyday interper-
sonal relationships was wrong.

Don grew up with unpredictable and conditional love.
From his earliest childhood he was given to understand:
"You will be loved IF . . ." "We will accept and approve of
you WHEN . . ." He grew up feeling that he never pleased
his parents.

Don came to see me as a young adult in his 30s because his depressions were becoming more frequent, lasting
longer, and were more frightening. Some well-meaning
Christian friends told him his problem was spiritual. "Truly
Spirit-filled Christians shouldn't have such feelings. They
should always feel joyful." This left Don with a double burden: his problem, and his guilt because he had the problem.

Don and I spent many hours together. It wasn't easy
for him to understand and accept God's love and grace, let
alone to feel it at the gut level. Because every experience of
relationships from childhood to adulthood contradicted
grace and love, it was hard for him to believe and feel
God's grace.

And Don had added to his problem. During those
down times, he had entered into wrong relationships with
the opposite sex. He would use this girl, and then that one,
to help him pull out of his depression. That was sin and he
knew it. Such misuse of another person added to his guilt,
so there was real guilt on top of his pseudoguilt. Again and
again he had gone through the whole cycle of tears, repentance, salvation, and renewed promises, only to break
them later.

Our process together took more than a year. But during this time there was healing of many painful memories and reprogramming of wrong ways of coping. He did his homework well, kept an honest journal of his feelings, read good books and listened to tapes, memorized many Scripture passages, and spent time in specific and positive prayer.

Some of the relearning took place in our relationship. He tried many, many times to maneuver me into rejecting him and withdrawing my loving acceptance of him. Don was trying to get me to behave the way his mom and dad did and the way he thought God did.

Healing didn't happen overnight, but thank God, it happened. Slowly, but surely, Don discovered grace in God's incredible and unconditional acceptance of him as a person. His down times began to come less frequently. He didn't work at getting rid of them, they just left—like dead leaves fall off the tree in the springtime when the new leaves come. He gained more control over his thoughts and his actions. His depressions began to lift, until now he has the normal ups and downs we all have.

Whenever I see Don alone, he smiles and says, "Doc, it's still too good to be true, but it's true!" That's the message. The trouble with the perfectionist is that he has been programmed to think it is too good to be true. You too may think: Of course, I believe in grace, but . . .

"Come to me," said Jesus, "all you who are weary and burdened, and I will give you rest" (Matthew 11:28). Isn't that good news? You don't have to live the way you do, for there's a better way to live! "I will give you rest. Take *my* yoke upon you . . . For my yoke is easy and my burden is light" (vv. 28*b*-30, emphasis added).

"My yoke is easy." What does that mean? His yoke is comfortable, because it is tailor-made to your personality, your individuality, and your humanity. "My burden is light" means that the Christ who fits you with a yoke will never leave you to pull the plow alone. He will always be yoked with you in the form of the One who comes alongside to help you carry that comfortable burden and yoke.

Notice the words of Charles Wesley's hymn as he traced the progression of God's healing grace in a guilt-ridden, perfectionist's heart.

Arise, My Soul, Arise

Arise, my soul, arise. Shake off thy guilty fears.
The bleeding Sacrifice In my behalf appears.
Before the throne my Surety stands,
Before the throne my Surety stands;
My name is written on His hands.

He ever lives above For me to intercede,
His all-redeeming love, His precious blood to plead.
His blood atoned for all our race,
His blood atoned for all our race,
And sprinkles now the throne of grace.

Five bleeding wounds He bears, Received on Calvary.
They pour effectual prayers; They strongly plead for me.
"Forgive him, oh, forgive," they cry.
"Forgive him, oh, forgive," they cry,
"Nor let that ransomed sinner die."

The Father hears Him pray, His dear Anointed One;
He cannot turn away The presence of His Son.
His Spirit answers to the Blood,
His Spirit answers to the Blood,
And tells me I am born of God.

My God is reconciled; His pard'ning voice I hear.
He owns me for His child; I can no longer fear.
With confidence I now draw nigh,
With confidence I now draw nigh,
And, "Father, Abba, Father," cry.

Background Scripture: Matthew 11:28-30; Colossians 2:8, 18-23

David A. Seamands has recently retired as professor of pastoral ministry, Asbury Theological Seminary, Wilmore, Ky. He served also as a missionary, then pastor, for the United Methodist church. This chapter is reprinted from *Healing for Damaged Emotions,* by David A. Seamands, published by Victor Books (1981, 1991), SP Publications, Wheaton, IL 60187.

Christians Need to Learn How to Confess Sin

by Dana Walling

THIS IS GOING TO SOUND BIZARRE. But it's a true story about a friend of mine.

He was an ordained minister who had committed adultery. The affair was a onetime experience that he and the woman realized was a big mistake. So the relationship ended immediately, but the guilt continued.

My friend, unable to talk himself into confessing his sin to either his wife or his supervisor, found himself sitting one day on the edge of a cliff overlooking the Pacific Ocean. One hundred feet below him emerald waves churned into a white froth crashing onto cobbled stones along the shore.

For the first time in his thirtysomething-year-old life, he found himself fighting the urge to commit suicide. With just the slightest twitch he could be over the edge. He prayed the cliff would crumble and do the job for him. At least then it wouldn't be his fault.

He conjured up the headlines, "Cliffs Claim Local Pastor in Tragic Fall." The papers would never have to know that the real fall had taken place months earlier.

In his first year as pastor of a small home mission

church he had seen God do great things. At district assembly his church received many awards. My friend began to see himself as successful and even invincible. This sense of invincibility soon crumbled: he sinned against God, the church, and everyone who loved and trusted him.

Sitting there on the cliffs, no other option seemed acceptable. The short pain of a fall seemed better than the long-term pain of living with this sin.

Hell became real as he contemplated life without the intimate relationship with Jesus he had depended on for so many years. Gone, too, was his career and his sense of self-respect. The anguish of the moment paralyzed him as he thought about never seeing his family again.

It's better this way, he thought. Now they'll never know the awful truth of my sin.

What stopped him? This is where the story gets bizarre. He found himself praying a prayer from Henri Nouwen's little book *The Way of the Heart,* "Lord Jesus Christ, have mercy on me a sinner!" The prayer originally comes from Luke 18:13.

As soon as my friend muttered that prayer, he had what he doesn't know how to describe except to call it a vision. My friend is not given to visions. This was a unique experience.

"I saw the ocean floor rise up," he told me. "And suddenly Christ was standing in front of me with outstretched arms. The imagery was powerful. It was as if Christ had leveled the ground in front of me, removing the threat. There was no cliff to jump from anymore. There was only a Savior with scars of forgiveness extended on my behalf."

Heaving sobs gripped my friend as he cried, "But, Lord, my sin! O God! My sin!"

Jesus merely nodded and said, "I know. It kills me too. Let My death be your death."

In that moment the young pastor found restoration. He told me, "The living hell of a broken relationship with the Lord was over. I knew I could face anything else because that relationship with Jesus was restored. I walked away from the cliffs filled with the Holy Spirit."

From his description of the next few minutes, the newspaper headlines could have read, "Local Pastor Seen Dancing on Cliffs."

The days after that happy episode of confession and restored relationship have been far from painless. My friend had to confess to his wife and his district superintendent. But when he did, he was met with compassion and healing. He is still enjoying life with his wife and young children. He had to surrender his credentials, but he has followed the church's path to restoration and is again serving in full-time ministry, though he has chosen not to pastor a church at this time.

We Holiness Christians Hate to Confess Sins

I've been profoundly influenced by what happened to my friend. And his experience has led me to believe that the discipline of confession is a God-given gift.

Those of us in the Wesleyan theological camp don't like to admit we sin. So we bottle it up inside, like my friend did. Or we call it something else; it wasn't a sin, it was a "mistake."

We create monsters by keeping our sins bottled up when the simple act of confession would turn our defeat to victory. And the more we explain our sins away as "character flaws," "mistakes," or "errors in judgment," the bigger the joy-stealing monsters grow.

The near tragedy of that day on the cliffs lies in the fact that my friend almost chose suicide over confession. The further tragedy is that too many Christians commit spiritual suicide, harboring unconfessed sin inside their carefully constructed, spiritually camouflaged shells.

Why do we hate to confess our sins?

One reason is our doctrine. Not that we don't believe in confession, but in our church we place great emphasis on entire sanctification. It is often called our "cardinal doctrine" or "doctrinal distinctive." As important as the concept of entire sanctification is to us, it has also been presented in some very confusing and misleading ways.

So what do we mean when we say entire sanctification? Simply, sanctification is the cleansing and filling work of God that begins—and continues—when a believer agrees to put God first. There are those who make this definition more complex and introduce confusing theological terms, but I look on it this way:

Our Part:	**God's Part:**
(with the help	*(through the*
of the Holy Spirit)	*Holy Spirit)*
Commitment	Cleansing
Obedience	Filling

Our problem begins when we understand that in sanctifying the believer, God cleanses us of our desire to sin—the root of sin, some call it. That illustration confuses some believers. And it leads them to believe that if the root is gone, it must be impossible for a sanctified believer to sin. After all, how can sin grow if there's no root? Illustrations are human attempts to explain heavenly truths. You can take illustrations only so far before they break down. The "root" illustration breaks down when you start talking about sin in the life of the sanctified.

As long as we have thoughts, desires, senses, as long as we have the ability to choose, we will have the opportunity to sin. As sanctified believers, we don't want to sin. And the

Holy Spirit works to protect us from sin. But even as sancti-fied Christians we have to continually submit to the Spirit's control. And when we don't—when we fail to recognize the Spirit's leading or when we find ourselves resisting it—we can only call what we do by its proper name: sin.

Does that mean we forfeit our sanctification? Do we have to go back to the spiritual starting line and begin the race again, revisiting the landmarks of regeneration and sanctification? The discipline of confession says no. We get back on the road at the place we pulled off.

The Holy Spirit does not abandon us. The Spirit's work merely changes from Counselor to Convictor. As soon as we confess, our spiritual journey can continue.

Ongoing confession in the Christian life does the same thing as those little bumps between the lanes on the inter-state: it keeps us on the right track. The Jesus whose death provides forgiveness for our sins is the same Jesus who de-fends us before the Father when we sin again (1 John 2:1). And the Holy Spirit who convicts of sin, and counsels us in daily life, is the same Holy Spirit who continues to convict us if we sin again.

The work of Jesus and the work of the Spirit seek to fulfill the Father's desire of "not wanting anyone to perish, but everyone to come to repentance" (2 Peter 3:9).

German theologian Dieter Fürst wrote, "Confession is a sign of repentance and thus a mark of the new life of faith." It is also the mark of the Spirit-filled believer. To paraphrase what Nazarene General Superintendent Dr. John Knight has written, the mark of the Spirit-filled per-son is seen in the short amount of time it takes to respond to the Spirit's touch in our lives. Even when we have mo-mentarily snatched our will from the Spirit's control, the sanctified believer is not at war with God. The sooner we return to the Lord, the better.

How Christians Can Confess Sin

Here are some guidelines I think could help us make room in our lives for the discipline of confession.

1. Confess first to God. We should confess sin only when the Holy Spirit convicts us about a specific act of disobedience to God. Later we can confess the sin to others as the Holy Spirit directs.

2. Keep public confession close to home. The military uses a phrase called "need to know." It means that details of an operation are revealed only to those who absolutely need that information. Those who have a greater responsibility have more detailed information than those who have less responsibility. The general will be informed of all aspects of a military plan. A private may be told only one part of the plan.

This is how it should be with our confession of sin. Most people in the church don't need to know the full details of a particular sin. You can tell the congregation God has dealt with you about it, and you are praising Him for delivering you from it. Those closest to you can be entrusted with more details to help hold you accountable so that you don't fall into the same trap again.

3. Telling no one the details is as dangerous as telling everyone. If we keep our confessions vague, we can end up hiding behind a fake spiritual respectability. And we can develop a destructive secret life of sin, which no one knows about because we keep it hidden behind our thin spiritual veneer.

It is essential that someone trustworthy know the full story.

4. Avoid overconfessing. Theology professor Richard Howard, now retired from Southern Nazarene University, taught about the difference between conviction and condemnation.

Conviction comes from the Holy Spirit to alert us to specific acts of sin. Our response to conviction should be to confess the sin, deal with it, and move on.

Condemnation comes from Satan to remind us of our failures in general. Satan's goal is to defeat us with a depressing feeling that we can never measure up to God's standards and that we are less spiritual than others. It constantly reminds us of past sins and tries to convince us that every strong emotion or tempting thought we experience is sin.

Condemnation leads to overconfessing. We spend too much time thinking about how inadequate we are, and we tell others to the point that we start boring them or getting on their nerves. The best principle is confess only when the Holy Spirit points to some specific sin in our life. And then we should confess only to those who are a part of the problem or a part of the solution.

5. A small group is a helpful place to confess. When John Wesley began to organize his Methodist societies, confession played an important role in these small groups. Many churches today use small-group meetings to build fellowship and accountability in the church.

This can be a perfect place for public confession. The people in the small group probably know and love you more than others, and they can do a better job of holding you accountable for taking steps to avoid repeating a particular sin. Such small groups must be centered in God's Word, accountable to the larger church body, and not an exclusive clique. The members need to be willing to tell others about the less flattering aspects of their lives. And they need to know how to keep a confidence.

The group should have the same goal as the Holy Spirit in dealing with a confession of sin: complete restoration as quickly as possible. A healthy small group is the best place I can think of for confession to take place.

No one who has felt the joy of being filled with God's Spirit wants to trade that for the sick-to-your-stomach feeling of sin. Yet, if we are honest about it, there are times when we do trip, stumble, fall, blow it, mess up, goof, and any of the other creative terms we use for sin. The light bulb of our joy goes out, and we slip into a dark spiritual depression.

None of us wants this to happen, but at times it does. God doesn't want us to sin, either. That's why He commands us to be holy. And that's why the Holy Spirit came to provide the power over sin that we need. But God also knows us better than we know ourselves. God knows we sometimes do what we don't want to do. So the Spirit who works to keep us from sin is the same Spirit who convicts us when we do sin. And God has paved the way for our restoration through the gift of confession.

Christians can be perfect—perfectly yielded to God. We don't need to pretend anything more. Confession of sin in a believer—even in a sanctified believer—is essential to spiritual health.

Perhaps we can put it this way: sin hidden = grace forbidden; sin confessed = grace expressed.

We can help the church become the place of healing and restoration God intended it to be by confessing our own sins and by creating an atmosphere of encouragement and support for others who confess.

Until we do this, Christians like my friend will search for answers elsewhere.

Background Scripture: Psalm 32:1-5; James 5:13-16; 1 John 1:9

Dana Walling is director of campus ministries for Point Loma Nazarene College, San Diego.

—————————— 8 ——————————

How to Make Worship Something Other than Boring

by David Holdren

I'M A PASTOR, and I've heard a lot of reasons why people stop coming to worship services. There are five I hear most often.

"They're boring." That's perhaps the number one charge.

"They're irrelevant." That's related to boring because if what goes on has little to do with your needs and interests, you'll probably get bored and stop coming.

"The people ignore me."

"I get hassled." This could mean anything from getting asked to work in the church to getting kidded about coming late or not coming often enough.

"The people are hypocrites."

Disappointed by Worship

If we get really honest—more honest than some worship-leading pastors might feel comfortable with—we'd all probably admit we've been disappointed by some worship services.

God wasn't exalted. The congregation wasn't nourished. And the whole experience seemed dry, routine, pointless, and unrelated to life on this planet.

Why does this happen?

1. Maybe the problem is your neighbor in the pew. Sometimes worship gets spoiled by someone sitting near you—a person whose life outside the church does not match the holy piety on display in church.

Watching a person like that pray and testify can make you a little sick to your stomach.

Reminds me of a poem.

I don't know who wrote it, but the poet sounds like someone with more than just a casual knowledge of life in the local church.

> *Worshiping above with saints we love,*
> *Oh, that will be glory;*
> *But worshiping below with folks we know,*
> *Now that's another story!*

If you worship with pew neighbors you think should be swallowed up into the bowels of the fiery earth, I have just one piece of advice.

Remember that you may be sitting and standing together in worship, but you stand individually before God. You are accountable only for yourself.

2. Maybe the problem is your worship leaders. Perhaps they don't seem prepared. And maybe they aren't. I'm a worship leader, and I know there have been times I wished I was somewhere other than on the platform.

Anywhere else would have been nice. Hidden in among the worshipers somewhere in the middle of the sanctuary. Home in bed. In a pit in Africa.

Any parents of teenagers know exactly what I mean. My wife and I raised two daughters who are now young adults. But I clearly remember many late, long, anguished Saturday nights when tempers flared at the Holdren homestead.

More than once this was because of broken curfews. A daughter would be out somewhere long past the curfew we agreed on, and my wife and I would lie awake waiting for her to return. We didn't know whether to be angry or worried, so we were usually both. Sometimes there were legitimate excuses, like a minor car wreck. Other times our daughter had just gotten into the wrong crowd. There were even a couple of rugged scenes in which we had someone packing a suitcase to leave home.

It seemed these family explosions always happened late Saturday night or in the early hours of Sunday morning.

Only a few short hours later I would be responsible for leading a congregation to worship and delivering God's Word to them. But I was emotionally drained and spiritually demoralized. I think you can understand why a pit in Africa would look attractive.

You know what Sunday morning can be like at your house. Parents contending with grumpy, resistant kids. Kids contending with grumpy, bossy parents. Spouses arguing over whether the dress makes her look too fat or if his favorite slacks belong in the rag pile.

Worship leaders have Sundays like that too.

They can also have other problems. They can be stuck with their own limited worship experiences, so the services can become exercises in monotony rather than creative adventures that energize the hour.

And the worship leaders can get so busy (or comfortable) that they don't take the time to plan the worship service well—or their sermon, for that matter.

So as a pastor I have to admit we can be part of the problem. But from one human to another, I'd ask you to err on the side of compassion toward your worship leaders. And if you were in my congregation, I'd invite your ideas for ways we might make the worship service more meaningful.

3. Maybe the problem is yourself. Maybe you come to church unprepared for worship. When I found out I was going to be writing this chapter, I surveyed several dozen people, asking them how prepared they usually were for worship. On a scale of 0-10 the average score was 5.3—which translated to "kind of prepared."

Later, in a Bible study, I posed this question: Imagine you were privileged to meet with some high-level, high-visibility public figure. This is a person of great nobility and character, someone you greatly admire. You will have one hour with the person. How would you prepare for the meeting?

The people said they'd make the hour a high priority on their calendar; nothing but an emergency would bump it aside.

They said they would present their best self. They would be well-groomed and rested. They'd not rush around just before the meeting and wind up going into it feeling rushed, frazzled, and distracted.

They said, too, they would have in mind the things of concern they'd like to talk about.

Not a bad list on how to prepare for worship.

How to Worship

Let's say you've prepared for the worship experience. You didn't crowd the weekend. You organized the family Saturday night by making sure there were clean clothes, gas in the car, and that the keys were where you could find them. You got to bed at a decent hour. You got up early enough not to feel rushed. And during the week you've spent some time in devotions, thinking about your personal needs and seeking God's direction.

What next? What else can you do to make the most of the worship experience?

1. Get involved in the worship. Attend church as a giver, and you will be more likely to receive.

Take the initiative to speak to others. Introduce yourself to those you don't know. Contribute to the warmth and friendliness of your congregation. *Be* a blessing instead of just expecting one.

Involve yourself in the congregational music whether or not you can carry a tune. The Psalmist said, "Make a joyful *noise* unto the Lord" (100:1, KJV, emphasis added). You can do that. Join in the readings and the prayers. Give those efforts some gusto as a gift of gratitude to God.

Be a greeter or nursery worker, or volunteer in some practical way. Make Sunday your day to give of yourself.

Worship is not what we get from God, it is what we give to God. So when we're on our way home, the wrong question to ask is, "What did I get out of it?" The right question is, "How did I do?"

Jesus said God is on the lookout for those who will worship Him with zeal, sincerity, and openhearted honesty (John 4:23-24). Without these, worship is a dry experience.

Perhaps we're too immersed in an entertainment culture. Maybe that is why we are tempted to measure worship services against the professionalism and emotional stimulation we experience in blockbuster movies or award-winning plays. But if we give way to this temptation, the pursuit of God becomes the pursuit of gaud and glitz. And critics in the pews and behind the pulpit alike start rating the worship services as either poorly done or well-done shows.

2. Expect God to meet with you. Public worship is a group appointment with God. Arrive with expectation. Expect to receive some revelation for your life. Plan on finding something that applies to your life right now.

I know that can be hard—especially if you have teenagers. But take it from Dad, we need to worship even when we don't feel like it. Even when life is in chaos, we need to keep doing the things we know are right and good. We need to do these things, such as worship, not only for ourselves but also for a God who deserves it.

Because your life is forever changing, look at every worship service as a fresh experience. Life for you is not exactly as it was last week or as it will be next week. The needs in your life and in those around you are unique each time you meet for worship. Rarely does the exact combination of worshipers ever meet twice. Each experience of worship is, indeed, a rare and divine moment to capture.

It's a time in which God reveals himself to us. It's a time we can take a hard and long look inward and respond. And it's a time we can fellowship with and draw strength from our spiritual family.

3. Extend your worship beyond the church and into life. Many Christians leave their experiences of worship at the church door when they head for the parking lot. But worship can come to life when we take it with us. I can remember times I spent surveying the beauty of nature where an inward sense of awe reinforced within me the majesty of the Creator.

I remember standing beside my wife at the birth of my children; silently watching at the bedside of a friend as he took his last breath; listening to an experience that has forever traumatized someone; looking at photographs of the dying and dead of the Jewish Holocaust. All these experiences usher me into profound moments of spiritual anguish, sadness, awe, or appreciation. They put me in touch with my Maker, Redeemer, and Friend. This, too, is worship.

Developing the holy habit of worship takes preparation and pursuit. But it produces spiritual stability, and it ignites a renewal of spiritual zest along our life journey in Christ.

I believe those who develop the discipline of worship as a gift *to* God are the same people who will be blessed by worship as a gift *from* God.

Background Scripture: Psalm 95:1-6; John 4:21-24; Hebrews 10:19-25

David Holdren is pastor of Cypress Wesleyan Church, Galloway, Ohio.

9

Restoring Zest to a Stale Prayer Life

by Dan Boone

KAREN came to my office upset. A year ago she had prayed and fasted for her mother, who was critically ill. But her mother died.

Since then, Karen's prayer life had been like a lonely walk through the desert. She wanted to know why. So she came to her pastor for advice.

I suggested she tell God about her feelings. It was not a welcomed idea.

"Tell God?" she replied. "I can't tell God I am angry at Him because He let my mother die!"

"Why not?"

"Because you don't tell God things like that."

When I asked what Karen did talk with God about, I discovered her prayers had been polite monologues, full of religious language, pious phrases, and empty repetitions. But there was no heart in her prayers.

I recognized the symptoms of an age-old prayer disease I call "nice-itis." Its symptoms are easy to spot. The patient:

● believes God isn't interested in knowing how we really feel about life

- is disappointed because prayer has not produced a noticeable difference
- prays predictable prayers over and over

A typical prayer of such a person might go something like this: "Father, thank You for this day. Help me to be a better Christian. Be with my children at school. Help us get the bills paid. I love You with all my heart. Amen."

Learning to Be Honest to God

Imagine Karen's surprise when I asked for the privilege of talking to God on her behalf and I prayed something like this.

"Father, I'm here with Karen. She is angry with You over the death of her mother. She hasn't been honest with You about that because she didn't think You permitted that kind of honesty. I think she's wrong about that. I talk to You constantly about things that bother me. You've never scolded me for being bluntly honest. I don't think You'll scold Karen either. Father, she's pretty dry inside right now. And she's not as close to You as she once was. She wants that to change. Would You help her restore honesty in praying? Amen."

Two gigantic eyeballs and one wide-opened mouth greeted my finished prayer.

"You mean you just talk to God like that?"

"Sure."

Karen isn't the only Christian who has found it hard to believe we can be honest with God. But it's true, God wants us to be honest with Him. Have you read the Psalms lately? Or how about Job? The Psalmist and Job were completely honest and frank with God about issues that upset them.

Psalms is a fantastic collection of songs and prayers. But it's more. It's a model of how to keep our prayer life vibrant.

The Book of Psalms, as we might expect, is full of praise and thanksgiving. About two-thirds of the psalms fall into this category. But there are also gripes and confessions and suggestions to God.

The Old Testament worshiper stayed alive by viewing God as a covenant partner who had made promises. Like Jacob, the Psalmist felt free to wrestle with God when it looked like He wasn't keeping His promises. Like Job, he felt if he could only get God in a court of law, he could win his case. And like Moses, he reminded God that everyone would judge His character by the way He treated His people.

Jacob, Job, Moses, and the Psalmist did not view prayer as pious monologues to a God who listened only for religious buzzwords. These men viewed prayer as a dynamic exchange of honesty between God and humanity. One rabbi in ancient times described Old Testament faith as "wrestling with God."

When our prayers start becoming cozy and comfortable, we are headed toward the desert.

Bible Writers Who Criticized God

The prayers of the Psalms are anything but complacent. They are punctuated with exclamation and question.

"How long, O LORD?[1] Will you forget me forever? How long will you hide your face from me? How long must I wrestle with my thoughts and every day have sorrow in my heart? How long will my enemy triumph over me?" (13:1-2).

Translation:

"Where are you, God?"

Or how about these two passages?

"I envied the arrogant when I saw the prosperity of the wicked. . . . Surely in vain have I kept my heart pure" (73:3, 13a).

"Remember how the enemy has mocked you, O LORD,
how foolish people have reviled your name" (74:18).
Translation:

"Can't you see what's going on down here?"

The Book of Psalms is full of passionate cries to God.
Psalm 37 is a cry that the wicked get the punishment they
deserve. Psalm 51 is a cry for cleansing after failure. Psalm
69 is a cry of desperation. Psalm 88 is a cry for God to come
out of hiding. Psalm 90 is a cry for God's favor. Psalm 109 is
a cry of revenge.

Some Old Testament believers refused to remain silent
when life seemed to fall below the promises of God.

So do many modern believers. Author David Well describes prayer this way. "It is, in essence, rebellion—rebellion against the world and its fallenness, the absolute and
undying refusal to accept as normal what is pervasively
abnormal. It is . . . the refusal of every agenda, every
scheme, every interpretation that is at odds with the norm
as originally established by God."[2]

We don't need to resign ourselves to dry prayer times.
We can pray about our prayers. Rather than sulk spiritually through the desert times, we can be honest with God.
We can express a holy discontent with the present and a
stubborn unwillingness to leave things as they are.

I wonder if God sometimes puts us in the desert to
help us see how badly we want zeal in our lives. If food is
taken from us, do we casually accept its loss and allow
ourselves to starve to death? Or do we declare our desire
to live?

Don't misunderstand me. I'm not saying we should
demand that God give us a greater sense of emotions in
our prayers. A prayer life that is only emotion-deep is too
shallow. God is not interested in pumping up His people
as we'd pump up a deflated tire. But He is stubbornly in-

terested in renewing us in His own image and likeness. We can call on Him all day long for a feel-good religion, and the answer will be no. But if we engage Him in conversation about our desire to be more like His Son, He will respond.

Giving God a List of Chores

I believe we can approach God boldly, but not in an arm-twisting ploy to get Him to do something for us. He is not our errand boy or go-fer. He is not the cosmic God-in-the-box who pops up when we turn the crank. He is not our bellhop or chauffeur.

He is God. He will not bend to our selfish demands.

He is sovereign. He will not let us call the shots.

But He has decided to include us in His purposes for the world. He has decided to act in us and through us. He has chosen us to be the embodiment of His Son on earth. And He has a passion for intimate relationship with us.

The Lord taught me a valuable lesson during the four years my daughter attended an inner-city school. On the mornings when I drove her to school, we would pray together in the car. My prayers sounded like a "to do" list for God.

"Keep her safe. Protect her from evil influences. Give her courage."

One day it occurred to me that God could work through her life to carry out His purposes for that school. So I began to pray, "Help her to be a leader for You. Give her courage to stand against wrong. Let her life influence other kids." As my daughter and I began to see her in partnership with God, a whole new way of praying emerged. We prayed about the evil in the school, the ways people spoke to each other, the disrespect for authority. We asked God to do something about it, and offered to be part of His plan.

I believe God prefers this to a list of daily chores.

The secret to finding zeal in our prayer life lies somewhere between the blunt honesty of pesky petitions and the sovereign will of God.

More Problems, More Solutions

I've tried to spotlight two major factors that produce dryness in prayer time: (1) nice prayers by nice people who say only what they think is on the preapproved prayer list, and (2) the failure to view prayer as involvement in God's plan to renew human beings in Christlikeness.

These are not the only causes of dryness. Just a few of the others are: stress, chemical imbalance, diet, unrealistic expectations, unconfessed sin, lack of discipline, loneliness, depression.

When these are the cause of desert dryness in the soul, it does no good to run harder or faster. Healing and help are needed from caring people, such as pastors, physicians, or Christian counselors.

No matter what is causing the spiritual dryness, though, we can keep on praying. The will to keep praying when zeal is far away is an act of faith. We know God is there. We know He cares. So we pray on. Like a slumping batter, we adjust our stance and grip, we try a new bat, we ask for coaching—whatever it takes to get back in the groove. But we keep praying.

Keeping a journal, or spiritual diary, gives us the chance to write our prayers in thoughtful sentences. Conversational prayer with friends involves us in new perspectives. Reading written prayers allows the saints of the ages to form our words for us. Praying the Psalms connects us with the passions of God's people. Singing our prayers focuses on the beauty of creative expression.

When prayer life gets routine, different styles of praying help us break out of a slump. But there is one indispensable ingredient that has nothing to do with the methods we try out.

That vital ingredient is the deep belief that God is active in the lives of those who pray. It's a belief that reminds us that no matter how we feel, we should pray on. For God is there.

1. LORD is in capital and small capital letters because it translates the personal name of God. It is the name God used of himself at the burning bush with Moses. So it is the name Old Testament writers used when they wanted to emphasize God as the One who had a unique covenant with Israel and who would be the nation's Deliverer, Protector, and Ruler.

2. David Wells, "Prayer: Rebelling Against the Status Quo," *Christianity Today,* Nov. 2, 1979, 33.

Background Scripture: Psalm 13; Matthew 7:7-10; Hebrews 4:16

Dan Boone is senior pastor of College Church of the Nazarene, Kankakee, Ill.

10

If Only . . .

by Scott Morton

AS I SAT AT MY DESK THAT DAY, I realized I was angry. It was a familiar feeling. I argued a lot. Not out loud, but mentally. Usually with people from the past. Usually angrily. And I always had the last word.

Around people I was cheerful and easy to talk to. But alone I was heavy in spirit. My wife said she loved to hear me laugh wholeheartedly because I did it so infrequently.

This was the pattern of my life: Every five or six weeks I'd find myself in a trough of discouragement for two or three days. Grumpy. Moody. Unable to sleep. Sometimes on the verge of tears. There had to be a reason.

So, despite the pressing deadlines of the work on my desk, I went to my favorite pizza joint to reflect on my lack of joy.

My thoughts went back to college days. As a senior I had been drafted by the Baltimore Orioles and the Minnesota Twins. But I gave up the opportunity to play professional baseball to enter Christian ministry.

Looking back, I realized that my decision was made hastily. I had neglected to ask the "why" questions. I had glorified the role of "full-time Christian service" and was in a hurry to get there. Counsel from others extolled the virtue of Christian work, but no one except the pro scouts extolled the virtues of baseball.

Morbid "if only" scenes rushed through my mind. I daydreamed about how great I would have been—striking out Reggie Jackson, winning 20 games year after year, setting records for strikeouts and complete games, and probably walks. And the testimony I could have had for the Lord—speaking engagements at sports banquets, testifying about Christ to the press, and on and on.

And the money! I saw myself giving hundreds of thousands of dollars to the work of God—to the applause of people.

Back to reality—my pizza was getting cold.

I knew daydreaming like this was self-centered, but I had been doing it for 15 years. I also knew God was sovereign, but somehow that knowledge didn't help me recapture my joy. Staying busy didn't help. Days off didn't help, and neither did successful ministry.

At first I thought bitterness was the problem. But I wasn't *that* hostile, just heavy in spirit. And I periodically experienced great joy in life and ministry. *Regret* is a better description of what I felt. Living a life of regret was robbing me of joy and fulfillment. I finally admitted to myself that the decision to get out of baseball to "serve the Lord" was the cause of my mood swings.

Out of desperation that day in the pizza parlor, I turned to the Bible. I didn't know where to start, so I began by looking up verses containing the word *bitter* and moved on to an in-depth study of regret. Over the next 24 months I discovered some practical insights for dealing with regret—the joylessness that comes when you focus on what might have been.

Identify the Source of Your Regret

Regret grows out of disappointment. In Genesis 27,

Esau experienced a severe disappointment: He was tricked out of receiving his father's blessing, and he lost the family inheritance. Instead of a life of power, wealth, and prestige, he believed he could look forward only to hard work and economic hardship. And he was furious.

In the Book of Ruth, Naomi's disappointment was over the death of her husband and sons. She would never know the joy of having grandchildren. She could expect only poverty. Widows without a family received what little they could gather from the corners of the grainfields or the few remaining olives and grapes after harvest. She was so distraught that she changed her name to Mara, which means "bitter."

Disappointment can stem from a tragedy, as in Naomi's case, or treachery, as in Esau's case. But it can also stem from a self-inflicted wound—a bad decision, a failure, or just plain sin—the scars of which we bear for years.

My disappointment stemmed from my career decision. I was disappointed at how hastily I had arrived at the decision to leave baseball. I should have thought it through more, I told myself. Maybe I had missed the will of God.

Recently, I came home from work feeling grumpy and angry. When this happens, I have learned from past experience to ask myself, "Have I had any disappointments, big or small, in the last few hours?" Sure enough, there were two that day—a confrontation with the accounting department on a trivial matter, and a minor failure to communicate clearly with a coworker.

Even the little disappointments—a frown from a friend, an argument with a child, a sarcastic remark from the boss, or even someone sounding a little cool on the phone—can become a breeding ground for regret unless the disappointments are specifically identified and surrendered to the Lord. Until then no amount of pep talks, Sunday sermons, or days off will lift the heaviness.

Forgive Yourself

When we have feelings of regret, usually the underlying cause is anger at ourselves. However, most regretful people point angry fingers at *other* people or circumstances, holding something or someone else responsible for their pain.

For years I blamed God, but it wasn't until I was caught in a snowstorm in a Chicago motel that I realized I needed to forgive the person who had hurt me the most—me! Alone in my room, with 24 hours of time on my hands, I invited "Scott, the hasty decision maker" to sit across the table from me. I looked at him and said, "I forgive you for all the hasty decisions, foolish sins, and lack of self-control you've displayed." And then I named one by one those incidents that I regretted most.

I felt a little foolish—like actor Jimmy Stewart talking to his imaginary six-foot rabbit, Harvey. But a burden was lifted that day. I felt new joy. In forgiving myself, I was also able to surrender once more to the Lord who had forgiven me years ago.

Don't Rehash the Past

If there could ever be a good reason for dwelling on what might have been, Joseph had one. Genesis 37 tells the story of his jealous brothers' conspiracy to kill him.

Put yourself in Joseph's place. You're coming to visit your family, but rather than greet you with open arms, they throw you into a pit and sell you to a band of traveling camel gypsies bound for Egypt. Now that's a disappointment.

In Genesis 41:51, Joseph says, "God has made me forget all my trouble and all my father's household." And to commemorate this, he named his first son Manasseh, which sounds like the Hebrew word for *forget*. Joseph could not have forgotten his troubles if he had continually rehashed them. I found that was just what I was doing. I often lived inside my head, condemning myself for bad decisions. I replayed past events day after day, digging up ways life would have been different if only I had changed this or that. *If only*. These mental arguments did no good. They only kept me feeling sorry for myself.

Trust God

"You intended to harm me, but God intended it for good to accomplish what is now being done, the saving of many lives" (Genesis 50:20).

Notice the phrase, "to accomplish what is now being done." Do you suppose Joseph would have accomplished as much good if he had remained in Israel, the 11th of 12 sons who were all sheepherders? He did much more for God in Egypt than he ever would have in his native land. The camel traders were God's vehicle to move him into an arena of larger service.

Joseph was able to see a greater purpose behind his hard times. Did he understand all God was doing? Probably not. But he trusted God and was therefore able to say, "It was not you who sent me here, but God" (Genesis 45:8).

Sometimes our regret centers around a real mistake—a sinful choice that has altered the course of our lives. But our God is a God of second chances. Throughout the Scriptures we see God advancing His kingdom through frail men and women, despite their foolish choices. He can even mold the fruit of our rebellion into a glorious feast as we surrender our lives to Him.

We all have regrets. Maybe it seems as if you're married to the wrong person, or stuck in the wrong job, or saddled with the wrong kids. Maybe you have a physical body you wouldn't have chosen. At times, we all dwell on what might have been.

I confess I still have days of defeat when regret wells up inside, especially when I realize that I'm no longer known as a "ballplayer." But the symptoms of discouragement—mental arguments and rehashing the past—are disappearing.

Increasingly I am coming to understand that I have been blessed and fruitful in ways I would never have imagined had I stayed in baseball. God continually confirms my calling to His service and that the decision I made in my 20s was no mistake.

But suppose it *was* a mistake; I could still rest in the assurance that God would not abandon me to the results of my failure. Nothing "in all creation," not our bad decisions or the results of others' failings in our lives, "will be able to separate us from the love of God" (Romans 8:39), or from His loving purposes for us. Let us put away the past, "forgetting what is behind and straining toward what is ahead" (Philippians 3:13*b*), looking forward to how our sovereign God will work in our lives.

Background Scripture: Genesis 50:15-20; Philippians 3:13b-14

Scott Morton is director of donor development at the Navigators' U.S. headquarters in Colorado Springs. The Navigators is an organization that helps Christians grow in the faith.

11

Laughter Makes the Heart Grow Fonder

by Annie Chapman

RECENTLY I MADE THE "MISTAKE" of taking my husband, Steve, shopping with me for a dress I needed for my 20-year high school reunion. As I held up each dress from the rack, Steve said, "That dress is too young for you."

After enduring these insults long enough, I moved to a rack of designer silk dresses and suits that Steve liked. But he wasn't looking at the price tags.

I told Steve, "Honey, you're absolutely right. I don't need to buy those *young, cheaper* dresses."

At that moment, Steve realized "mature" dresses cost a whole lot more than "younger," cotton ones. After he looked at the price tags, he decided I'd gotten younger while I was shopping.

Steve didn't realize his comments hurt my feelings. Of course, what he really meant was that he liked more classic styles. But by using humor, I made my point without accusing Steve of something he didn't mean.

Author Tim Hansel has observed that "humor has the unshakable ability to break life up into little pieces and make it livable. . . . Life really is fun, if we only give it a chance.

Countless moments of serendipity are waiting for us—if we have eyes to see, ears to hear, and hearts to respond."

There's no better gift we can give our family and friends than to "lighten up" and see the humor in our often all-too-serious lives. Here's why.

Laughter Is Hazardous to Your Illness

The Bible says, "A cheerful heart is good medicine" (Proverbs 17:22*a*). That fact has been verified by the medical profession. Psychologist David McClelland found that after a group of medical students watched a funny movie, the infection-fighting proteins in their bodies increased.

William F. Fry, M.D., of Stanford University, who has studied laughter for 30 years, calls it "inner jogging." He says a long, hearty laugh every day does your cardiovascular system as much good as 10 minutes of rowing. Sounds good to me! Laughing is more fun, and it doesn't require $150 shoes and a shower afterward!

Laughter seems to be God's provision for releasing the natural painkillers in your body that combat arthritis and slow down the release of stress-producing hormones. It may not be long before your doctor advises, "Forget the aspirin. Take two belly laughs and call me in the morning." Already nurses at Oregon Health Sciences University wear buttons proclaiming: "Warning—Humor may be hazardous to your illness."

It Breaks Up Fights

I grew up in a little community where everyone knew everyone else's business. To save himself some embarrassment, my dad arranged with our banker to cover any outstanding checks we kids wrote. Therefore, keeping a balanced checkbook was never a burning need for me because I always knew Daddy would make up the deficit. This worked well—that is, until I married. Steve made it clear he was my husband, not my father, and that from now on I'd need to take responsibility for recording the amount of money I parted with.

On the whole, I've done quite well at keeping my accounts in order. But I recently let things slide, and we got a call from the bank. When Steve came home from paying out several overdraft charges, he was in a bad mood, to say the least. And he told me exactly what was on his mind.

The problem was, he was dead right. So I could only agree with everything he said. When he was finished laying out his case, he leaned over, peered at me, and said, "Will this *ever* happen again?"

I looked back with the same seriousness. "Yes, it will," I told him, "but not for a long time."

The humor of that moment dispelled any further anger. We burst into laughter, then I promised to make a concerted effort to correct my ways.

Now, when we reflect back on that time, what we remember most is not the overdraft payment or my neglect of our finances, but the amusement of my response.

Of course, there's no place in marriage for "jokes" that put each other down. But there is room for wit to replace sarcasm or genuine fury. As we cultivate humor in our relationships, we sometimes need to see the lighter side in things other people say to or *about* us.

It Helps Us Cope with Bizarre People

One night after we had finished a concert, Steve and I changed into our traveling clothes and stopped at a fast-food restaurant before heading to the airport. A woman who had attended our concert came up to me in the restaurant to tell me how much she had enjoyed it. She went on to tell me something I could have lived without.

She said, "I was sitting in the balcony, and from a distance you looked young and pretty. But now that I see you up close, I see you're not."

How do you respond to that? "Thank you" seemed rather insincere. So I simply replied, "That's an interesting observation."

That wasn't the response she wanted, however—so she repeated her statement verbatim.

I smiled and simply said, "Thank you." That seemed to satisfy her.

I couldn't wait to tell Steve what had just happened. The humor wasn't in her thoughtless comment, but in her insistence that I thank her for it.

With Steve's receding hairline, he's had his share of wisecracks to deal with. One man said, "Steve, God really must love your face."

Steve eagerly asked, "What makes you say that?"

His friend replied, "Because He's clearing off a place for another one."

Humor is the spoonful of sugar that makes the experiences of life more palatable for us all.

It Makes the World a Brighter Place

In a world where every newscast burdens us with reports of rapes and murders and bombings, it's not easy to find the lighter side of life. We have a few ideas that may help.

● **Value those who help you laugh.** Solomon wisely said, "There is a time for everything . . . a time to weep and a time to laugh" (Ecclesiastes 3:1, 4). We have dear friends who make the zaniest home videos you can imagine. They dress up in costumes and put on these elaborate sitcoms. They live in Texas, and we live in Tennessee. Every once in a while we receive their latest production. We watch and laugh as we see how much their children have grown and catch up on what's new in their lives.

They can find humor in the most mundane of life's moments, and when we're with them, we find as much to laugh about as to cry about.

● **Collect laugh starters.** Steve and I have gotten hooked on the homespun stories of humorist Garrison Keillor, because every time we hear them, they tickle us. Some people we know save jokes and cartoons that make them giggle.

One of our favorite collection of "funny-bone ticklers" is taken from notices that have actually appeared in church bulletins. Feel free to add these to your collection:

1. This afternoon there will be a meeting at the north and south ends of the church. Children will be baptized at both ends.

2. This being Easter Sunday, we will ask Mrs. Johnson to come forward and lay an egg on the altar.

3. On Sunday a special collection will be taken up to defray the expense of a new carpet. Will those wishing to do something on the carpet please come forward and get a piece of paper.

4. Potluck supper: prayer and medication to follow.

5. Don't let worry kill you off—let the church help.

● **Look for ways to laugh when you don't feel like it.** Psychologist William James said, "We don't laugh because we're happy—we're happy because we laugh." I detect some Christian truth in that thought. For example, I don't always feel like reading the Bible, but when I do, the "want-to" usually follows.

It's the same with laughter. Life with Christ is full of joy, but I don't always feel that joy. Sometimes working to find the humor in my day uncorks the joy of the Lord that was in me all along.

When something makes you laugh, take it seriously. If a movie makes you laugh, buy your own copy—it's cheaper than a psychiatrist.

"Lighten up" is advice we need to take to heart for our sakes, our family, and all those who have to be around us.

Background Scripture: Proverbs 15:30; 17:22; Ecclesiastes 3:1, 4

Annie Chapman and her husband, Steve, are musicians. The chapter is adapted from *Gifts Your Kids Can't Break,* by Steve and Annie Chapman with Maureen Rank. Copyright 1991 Steve and Annie Chapman. Used by permission of Bethany House Publishers, Minneapolis, MN 55438. All rights reserved.

12

Your Physical Condition Can Affect Your Spiritual Life

by Gary Morsch, M.D.

RON SCRUGGS is a member of my Sunday School class. Not too long ago he had what I call the "ultimate surgery."

Surgeons can do a lot of incredible things. They can repair the brain, reattach amputated limbs, and bypass clogged arteries in the heart. Plastic surgeons can even take an aging face and make it look decades younger. But all these remarkable surgeries pale in comparison to the "ultimate surgery."

Ron first started showing symptoms when we were on a weekend mission project at the Manhattan Church of the Nazarene in New York City. In New York you have to walk a lot. And Ron found himself getting increasingly tired and short of breath. He saw his doctor when he got home and discovered he had a serious heart problem. His heart muscle was slowly deteriorating. There is no known cure, except the ultimate surgery—a heart transplant.

Ron spent many weeks in the intensive care unit as he waited for a new heart. He became weaker and weaker, to the point that all of us worried he might not live long enough for the hospital to find a donor. Ron experienced something during those long days that all of us experience from time to time: discouragement.

There were times he didn't know if he'd live through another day. Not only did he get discouraged, he became depressed. Some days he was too weak to pray. And there were times he felt spiritually isolated and far from God.

Ron's weakened heart, his depression, and the side effects of powerful medications left him feeling spiritually defeated.

But it was often in Ron's lowest moments that someone would call and offer an encouraging word and let him know they were praying for him. Ron says his spirit would soar, and a strength would rise up to carry him through another day.

Ron Scruggs finally had the ultimate surgery. Inside his chest today beats a new heart. But he has more than just a new heart. He has a new insight about his faith. He understands that no matter how bad he felt during the ordeal, his relationship with God never changed. The feelings might not have been there, but the relationship was, because God was.

Not only is our sense of spiritual vitality affected by our physical and emotional state, but also the opposite is just as true. Our physical and emotional health are also affected by our spiritual condition. The how and why is just now being appreciated by scientists.

Medical Science Is Rediscovering a Bible Truth

Though science is just beginning to unlock the secrets of this complex interaction, Scripture has been teaching it for thousands of years. Proverbs 14:30 says, "A heart at peace gives life to the body, but envy rots the bones."

Methodist founder John Wesley picked up on the idea too. In his 1759 journal he asked, "Why do not all physicians consider how bodily disorders are caused or influenced by the mind?"

Medicine has made incredible advances in our lifetime. We are treated today by an array of specialists. Not only is there a specialist for every organ of the body, there are superspecialists who deal with only one part of an organ or one disease. This is wonderful when you need that type of specialty care. But there are times we need an old-fashioned general practitioner who knows us and can take care of us as a whole person.

Medical science has continued to dissect the human body into smaller and smaller pieces—to the point that some have forgotten God created humans as a whole. We're not just a collection of organs stuck together and hung in a skeleton. God created us as unbelievably complicated beings consisting of physical, emotional, and spiritual dimensions, all interacting with each other. Perhaps it's no accident that the first and greatest commandment of Jesus seems to convey an awareness of this: "Love the Lord your God with all your heart and with all your soul and with all your mind" (Matthew 22:37).

Medical science is just starting to explore the connections between the body and the spirit. In fact, there is a new field of scientific research—psychoneuroimmunology—that deals with the connections between the mind, body, and spirit.

Scientists are investigating biochemical links between the mind and the immune system. Several studies have found that a positive, hopeful attitude can actually increase the kinds of immune cells that fight off infections and cancer. Other studies have found a link between religious faith and improved health.

These recent discoveries are proving what Ron experienced—that spiritual feelings are intricately intertwined with physical condition.

How Physical Problems Produce Spiritual Problems

There are many physical problems that affect our sense of spiritual vitality. In fact, anything that affects us physically can affect how we feel spiritually. But let's look at some of the more common problems.

1. Fatigue. Too many of us suffer this disease that grows out of busyness and overcommitment.

Some of the most common ways fatigue expresses itself in the body is through depression, hopelessness, and lack of motivation. When we burn the candle at both ends, we are inviting spiritual problems. It's difficult to summon the energy and motivation to give attention to a growing relationship with Christ when we're tired.

2. Stress. This is closely related to fatigue, but its impact on our health, and our spirituality, is even more profound.

Stress has to do with the way we react to difficult circumstances. Some people can handle a lot of stress. Others get stressed out when they are confronted by even the smallest of life's hassles. When we start to exceed our limit of stress, our body releases powerful hormones that can raise blood pressure, increase stomach acid, elevate cholesterol levels, and even decrease some immune system functions.

So stress can cause a multitude of physical problems, including high blood pressure, ulcers, heart disease, depression, and fatigue.

Through its damaging effects on the mind and the body, especially as it leads to fatigue or depression, stress can drain our sense of spiritual vitality.

3. Chronic disease. If we live long enough, all of us will eventually suffer from one kind of chronic disease or another.

The list seems endless and includes heart disease, diabetes, arthritis, cancer, and high blood pressure. Scientists are continuing to explore the biochemical link between body, mind, and spirit, and are finding that a disease that affects one dimension also affects the others, for better or worse.

Because chronic illnesses usually influence other organ systems, they have a profound impact on the total person—physically and spiritually.

4. Medication side effects. People suffering from chronic disease must often take powerful medications. Unfortunately, these medicines have powerful side effects.

Certain classes of medications have a greater potential for side effects. Medicines used in the treatment of high blood pressure are notorious for this; some of these drugs can produce depression. Even common over-the-counter drugs, like antihistamines and decongestants that are used for the treatment of allergies and colds, can cause fatigue, insomnia, anxiety, and even depression.

5. Chronic conflict. Our emotional and psychological condition is an important part of the whole person; it can affect both our physical and spiritual condition.

For example, unresolved anger, fear, and guilt can sap our spiritual energy. Chronic conflict of any kind, whether it's related to our marriage, children, job, or friends, can lead to spiritual fatigue, not to mention physical diseases.

6. Depression. One of the most spiritually devastating illnesses, depression, is also one of the most common. It affects up to 20 percent of the population, Christians and non-Christians alike.

Most doctors believe depression is a biochemical deficiency of brain hormones. It can produce profound physical and spiritual complications and is a major reason Christians feel spiritually defeated.

Too many Christians live in spiritual defeat simply because they suffer from undiagnosed depression. Many attribute their feelings of hopelessness, despair, and lack of motivation to a spiritual problem, when the real problem is depression. Unfortunately, many well-meaning Christians "spiritualize" the symptoms of depression and other emotional problems, rather than recognizing them for what they are—physical and emotional symptoms of a treatable disease.

But the fact is emotional problems are no more spiritual than cancer. And they need to be treated by professionals.

Many of the physical and emotional problems we face are lifelong conditions with little chance for complete cure. For the most part, we humans have to endure most of our ailments. And many of us have to take powerful medications with potent side effects.

How then can we maintain our sense of spiritual vitality with imperfect bodies?

How to Keep Physical Problems from Sapping Your Spirit

1. Accept the fact that your sense of spiritual vitality is affected by physical conditions. We must understand that feelings of spiritual fatigue, isolation, or defeat may not be due to spiritual failure, but to physical or emotional illnesses, or to side effects of treatments or medications.

God wants each of us to live as victorious Christians. To confuse physical and emotional symptoms as evidence of spiritual failure is one sure route to spiritual defeat.

2. Learn good nutritional habits. Eat less fats, cholesterol, and sweets, and maintain a proper weight.

3. Start exercising. Developing a regular exercise program will do unbelievable wonders for the whole person, not only by reducing the risk of chronic diseases, but also by reducing stress and depression, and positively affecting one's spiritual vitality.

Medical studies I've read have shown that exercise increases the levels of the hormones in the brain that produce feelings of hope and optimism. The "runner's high" really does exist; it occurs when powerful hormones are released into the brain during vigorous exercise.

So one of the best treatments for depression is exercise. In fact, since exercise has such positive effects on a person's emotional state, it follows that exercise will also have a positive effect on our sense of spiritual vitality.

4. Avoid unnecessary drugs. This includes excessive amounts of caffeine.

5. Maintain a regular schedule of preventive medical exams. This is to detect medical problems at a stage when they are more easily treated or cured. Find a doctor who will take the time to listen to you, answer your questions, and treat you as a whole person. If your doctor won't, find one who will.

6. Get counseling for emotional problems. Too many people believe that seeing a counselor, psychologist, or psychiatrist is a sign of weakness.

Is it a sign of weakness to see a medical doctor when you're sick?

If not, then why are so many people hesitant to see a pastor or counselor when they are experiencing psychological or emotional illness? God has provided Christians with a variety of tools to maintain the health of the whole person; it's important we use all the means available to become as healthy and whole as possible.

7. Keep a positive attitude. Science has recently been probing the powerful connection between attitude and the health of the whole person—physical, emotional, and spiritual. Though this connection may be new to 20th-century scientists, the writers of Scripture spoke of this truth many centuries ago in the Book of Proverbs: "A cheerful heart is good medicine, but a crushed spirit dries up the bones" (17:22).

Do the Best You Can with What You Have

Christians face the same physical and emotional illnesses that afflict the rest of the human race. Although we may try our best to maintain the highest levels of health in body and mind, we still suffer disease and illness.

How should we respond when the inevitable happens? Do we throw up our hands in despair? I believe in doing the best we can with what we have.

I often travel to different countries, and I've had many opportunities to practice medicine in situations that were less than ideal. But I've learned to do the best I can with what I have.

Several months ago I accompanied a group of Sunday School teachers on a study tour of Israel. On our last day there, as we were on our way to the airport, one of the tour members fell and injured her wrist. The lady was 69 years old, and she fell hard, so I was concerned she might have broken a bone. Knowing we didn't have time to go to an emergency room for an X ray, I splinted her arm, gave her some pain pills, and told her I thought she could wait until she returned home to get it treated.

As we were going through security at the Tel Aviv airport, I suddenly had an idea. Why not use the security X-ray machine to x-ray my patient's arm?

After I finally convinced the head of security, I carefully positioned the lady's arm inside the X-ray unit. But the security guard told me that wouldn't work. Whatever was to be x-rayed had to be moving along on the conveyor belt!

Fortunately, my patient was a good sport with a positive attitude. I helped her up onto the conveyor belt, positioned her with her arm outstretched in front of her, and away she went. I ran to the other end and caught her as she came through.

The X ray worked. My patient indeed had a fractured

wrist, but the bones were in good position, and she made her flight home.

Ideally, it would have been nice to have taken her to a "real" hospital for a "real" X ray. But we made do with what we had.

That is the best any of us can do. Each of us has certain physical and emotional characteristics—some we were born with, some that developed later; some good, some bad. As time goes by, many of us will be devastated by incapacitating disease or emotional illness. In many cases treatment will alleviate our illness but not cure it.

Even then, we don't have to despair. We can continually strive to make the best of what God has given us, to reach our potential as whole persons—physically, emotionally, and spiritually. As Paul says, "Whatever you do, do it all for the glory of God" (1 Corinthians 10:31).

Entering into a relationship with Christ is life's most important adventure. We set out on an exciting spiritual journey that lasts a lifetime. Though our relationship with God remains solid, we must continually work to maintain our sense of spiritual vitality.

Because God has created us as whole persons in which there is an interaction between body, mind, and spirit, we must seek to achieve and maintain the highest levels of vitality and wellness, not only spiritually but physically and emotionally as well.

Background Scripture: Proverbs 14:30; Matthew 22:34-40; 1 Corinthians 6:19-20

Gary Morsch is a physician who has a family practice in Olathe, Kans. He has traveled throughout the world on medical assignments for charitable organizations. And he has organized airlifts of medical supplies, most recently to Russia.

13

Holding On to Victory When Times Get Tough

by Carolyn Lunn

THE PLANE WAS NEARLY FULL that Monday morning, but I hoped the center seat beside me would stay empty. I was tired from a grueling summer schedule. I had spoken at seven conferences for pastors' wives in the last three months and was on my way to the eighth.

As I waited, a lovely woman in a gray, pin-striped suit stopped by my aisle seat. "I'm afraid I have the center seat," she said.

She spoke with a slight British accent, but she looked to be from Pakistan or India.

There wasn't much elbow room after she sat down, but both of us took work from our briefcases. She began to read a technical journal, and I began reviewing my speech notes and excerpts from my book, *Joy—Anyway: Seeing God in the Tough Times.* When I took out my Bible to check some scripture, she asked, "Are you a born-again believer?"

Surprised, I answered, "Yes, I am!"

"I used to be a Christian," she said. "But I seem to have lost my faith along the way. I noticed the title of your book. I assume it means you can have faith even when trouble and crisis come. Do you believe that?"

"That is what it means," I said. "Yes, I do believe it. I wrote this book." Startled, she looked me over a little more carefully as I continued. "The book is not just my story, but it is the principles I learned along the way—the things I believe God has taught me about himself."

"Well," she said, "I wasn't able to hang on to my faith."

She told me she was born in India but received her higher education in England. She had a doctorate in mathematics, a master's degree in science, and another master's in computer science. She was a teacher in a prestigious Ivy League school in Boston.

As we talked, I was impressed with how intelligent she was. I learned that her husband had his doctorate and also taught in a neighboring college of equal reputation. She had not met this man before her parents arranged the marriage. But she said she learned to love him.

Then her eyes grew troubled. With a bit of hesitation she explained that after her marriage, her family had caused the couple a great deal of pain, opposing them in different ways. It was obviously hard for her to speak of such personal things; she had an innate reserve about her. She did not go into any detail, but her hurt and bitterness were etched into her face.

She said, "I suppose just looking at me, you would say, 'She is a success. She has a fine education, position, prestige in her profession, a good marriage. She certainly has it altogether.' But you would not be able to see the pain, disillusionment, and despair inside of me. I have not been able to understand why God has allowed this devastation. My husband is a Muslim. Recently he has been deeply depressed because of the accusations hurled at him by my family. God has seemed so far away. My faith has been shattered. How have you been able to keep your faith?"

For the next two hours I opened the Bible and my book to tell her about some of the struggles I had faced.

I grew up in a Christian home, but I've faced some difficult times. As a result of complications during my birth my mother was often ill with a blood circulation problem in her legs. Many times she would have to stay off her feet until an ulcerated area healed. But at least this gave us plenty of time to talk. At the side of her bed I accepted Jesus as my Savior when I was eight years old.

In my sophomore year in college I met a young man who was a senior and called to the ministry. I fell in love with him, and after he graduated, we married, then moved to Kansas City so that he could attend seminary. We had been married only eight months when, on a weekend trip to Peoria, Ill., to visit my parents, we had a car accident. My husband was killed. Injured in the accident myself, I struggled with grief as I tried to rebuild my life.

As a young widow of 20, I returned to college and finished my degree in education. My struggle to feel like a whole person again spanned many years: beyond my college graduation, beyond my return to Kansas City to teach, beyond graduate school.

Five years after the accident I married Vernon Lunn, who had lost his first wife to cancer. He had two little girls, so I was suddenly about to become not only a bride but also a stepmother. My happy anticipation, however, was offset a bit by another reality. Just three weeks before we were to be married, Vernon's home burned to the ground. He had been renting it, completely furnished, to some people while he and the girls lived with his parents. One of the renters had been smoking on the couch, and some ashes got into the cushions, smoldered a while, then burst into flames. No one was hurt, but we lost the house and everything in it.

I told the lady flying with me about other crises in my life. The miscarriage of twin baby girls after five and a half months of pregnancy. My husband's times of unemployment. My bout with cancer, which resulted in a double mastectomy.

She listened intently, asking only a few questions. At times, we laughed together and cried together. Then I began to tell her how God led me to scriptures that told me of His love and faithfulness. And we talked about four lessons I learned through it all.

1. Heartache and pain come to everyone.

Christians aren't isolated from the pain life brings. We'd like to be. Or at least we'd like to understand why God is allowing us to endure such heartbreak.

Sometimes we eventually do see how God uses our suffering to help us or others around us. But often we never see the connection. It's there that understanding ends and trust begins.

As I struggled with my own pain after my husband died, the Holy Spirit seemed to remind me of a time when as a little girl I had listened to a Gideon speaker who came to our church to ask for support. He told of a hopeless, inebriated man in a lonely hotel room who picked up a Gospel of John on the nightstand. There this man read of God's mercy and love, and, confessing his sin to the Lord, found peace.

That memory led me to read the Book of John. In brokenness I cried, "Lord, help me to see You as I have never seen You before as I read the Book of John."

The senior girls at my college lived in small, ranch-style homes converted for use by eight girls and a resident counselor. The rooms were small, and privacy was scarce. Many times I would slip into the bathroom after everyone had gone to bed, to find light so that I could read John without disturbing anyone's sleep.

I believe God is with me all the time, but I sensed His presence in a unique way when I got to John 20:30-31. It was then the Lord stamped peace indelibly on my heart.

"But these are written, that ye might believe that Jesus is the Christ, the Son of God; and that believing ye might have life through his name" (KJV).

Hope leaped into my heart and brought joy along as company. For suddenly I saw Jesus in a new way. I saw Him in His sovereignty, His suffering, His love for those He met each day, and His power as the ministering Messiah. And I realized I could walk right up to reality—any reality—and He would meet me there.

2. The purpose of our life is to know God.

The apostle Paul says, in Philippians 3:10, "I want to know Christ and the power of his resurrection and the fellowship of sharing in his sufferings, becoming like him in his death."

The image we have of God is the most important fact of our lives. It affects, and often controls, our response to every reality we face. If our concept of God is the image revealed in Scripture, we will live lives of hope and healing. But if our image is distorted, we will live with despair and hopelessness.

If we know the God of Scripture, we learn that He is trustworthy. We can depend on Him in the way a child can depend on a loving father or mother. After my first husband died, I realized I had depended too much on his close relationship with God and the insights he had learned; I had not nurtured my own intimate relationship with God. So when a crisis came, my concept of God was underdeveloped. I had to study His Word to see who He was so that I could discover the truth that would enable me to trust Him. We cannot trust someone we do not know.

Christian author Oswald Chambers says one of God's greatest desires is to help us *unlearn* things that hinder us from truly knowing Him. One thing many need to unlearn is that God is a cosmic errand boy we can demand to do our will. Instead of teaching us how to get what we want, God wants to teach us how we can learn to listen for His will. That's because in His will joy and adventure await us.

3. Don't endure trouble, use it.

Christian writer and minister E. Stanley Jones said, "Jesus took the worst thing that could happen to Him, namely, the cross, and turned it into the best thing that could happen to humanity, namely, its redemption. He didn't bear the cross; He used it. The cross was sin, and He turned it into the healing of sin; the cross was hate, and he turned it into a revelation of love; the cross was man at his worst, and Jesus turned it into God at His redemptive best.

"Take whatever happens—justice and injustice, pleasure and pain, compliment and criticism—take it up into the purpose of your life and make something of it. Turn it into a testimony! Don't explain evil; exploit evil; make it serve you."*

As a young child I was sexually abused by a baby-sitter. The devastating impact on my life created intense feelings of victimization. But in the last six years, God has been leading me to healing.

Not only is God helping me cope with the pain of what happened, but also I believe He is going to give me the ability to help others who are hurting because of abuse.

4. We choose how to respond to life.

No one else can determine for us the attitudes we will carry around throughout our life. It is our responsibility. We may have experienced life at its most unfair, and we may want to blame these hard times for shaping our attitudes. But as one who has faced a fair share of heartache, I've discovered that with God's help we really can control how we respond.

When I was a senior in college, another senior girl started a false rumor about me. I can't remember what the rumor was, but I remember getting upset and wondering how the lie might hurt those whom God had been able to help through my Christian testimony. I had been very active in campus ministries during those college years, so I feared some people might get disenchanted, not only with me but with God too.

I first learned of this rumor the day the girl confessed to me and asked for forgiveness.

My first reaction was tremendous hurt and despair. I did not even know this girl well. Why would she do this to me?

As I tried to think about how to respond, I silently cried out to God for help. I needed to say something to the girl, but with my feelings so raw, I needed God to give me the words.

Tears were running down my cheeks, and my throat was constricting. I could barely say anything, but I finally managed to ask her to go to those she had told the lies to and confess her dishonesty. She agreed. Then I told her that with God's help I would forgive her.

God's grace did just that. He has so wiped the experience out of my life that I cannot even remember the girl's name now. I chose to focus on God's will and not the problem, and I have never regretted it. It was a valuable lesson.

All around us are people living in quiet desperation, wondering, Where is God in all this? They are confused, hurting, and crying alone. You cannot tell it by their outward appearance. But inside, where no one but God can see, they feel insignificant, lonely, and helpless.

My airplane friend from India and I finished our conversation as we landed in San Diego. No longer were we strangers to one another. She asked me to send her a book so that she could think more about the ideas we had discussed. As we gathered our things together to get off the plane, she said, "Do you think God put us together on the plane today? I feel that He did."

"Yes," I said, "I believe it was a divine appointment."

She promised me she would write and let me know her reaction to all we had talked about. She followed me to the baggage claim area and seemed reluctant to leave. But when it was time to go, I gave her a hug and said, "I'll be praying for you, but remember—the choice is up to you. You can have joy anyway."

---

*E. Stanley Jones, *Song of Ascents* (Nashville and New York: Abingdon Press, 1968), 180.

Background Scripture: Proverbs 3:5-6; John 20:30-31; Philippians 3:10; 1 Peter 1:3-9

Carolyn Lunn is a frequent speaker at church leadership conferences, author of *Joy—Anyway* (Beacon Hill Press of Kansas City), and mother of three children. She lives with her husband in Olathe, Kans.

THE DIALOG SERIES

For a description of all available Dialog Series books, including some that may not be listed here, ask for a free brochure from your favorite Christian bookstore, your denominational distributor, or Beacon Hill Press of Kansas City.